ROOFS OVER

A GUIDE TO OREGON'S COVERED BRIDGES

BY NICK AND BILL COCKRELL
MAPS AND DRAWINGS BY SHERYL COCKRELL

I.S.B.N.—0-911518-50-9

Copyright© 1978 by
M. Wayne Cockrell and William Cockrell

Printed in the United States of America

THE TOUCHSTONE PRESS
P.O. Box 81
Beaverton, Oregon 97005

Dedication

This book is dedicated to the men who built Oregon's covered bridges and to the individuals who are working to preserve the structures as reminders of the persevering spirit of Oregon's early settlers.

Acknowledgements

A volume so rich in historical detail has involved the efforts of a number of people who have given their time and energy to make the information contained herein as accurate as possible. We would like to express our appreciation to the following people for their willingness to aid in our research for information:

Ralph Howe, retired Polk County surveyor, and Ray Boydston, retired Dallas Water Company employee, for data on early Polk County bridges; Dave Morgan and Morris Cook, Benton County Public Works Department, for information on Benton County covered bridges; Del Burkhart and Neal Michael, Linn County Engineer's office, for details on Linn County bridges; John Anderson, Marion County director of Public Works, for a historical perspective of Marion County covered spans; Lavola Bakken, Douglas County historian, Don Anderson, Douglas County Engineer's office, and George Abdill, Douglas County Museum, for details of Douglas County bridges; Larry Olsen, Lane County surveyor, John Smeed, Environmental Section of the Lane County Road Department, and Chuck Angemeir, Lane County Bridge Section, for their valuable information on Lane County's covered spans; Richard Donovan, National Society for the Preservation of Covered Bridges, for furnishing material on guide numbers for covered spans; John Mingus, Georgia Pacific Corporation, for supplying data regarding the covered railroad bridges in Coos County; Harold Robinson, Coos County bridge superintendent, and Curt Beckham, Coos County resident, for supplying details on the history of bridge construction in Coos County; Bill Bowers, for relating his efforts to construct the Rock 'O the Range Bridge; Irene Hammer, research analyst, Right-of-Way Section, and Bill De Souza, bridge engineer, Oregon Department of Transportation, for probing old files for photographs and blueprints of early covered bridges; Paul Hartwig and Robert Sutton, State Historic Preservation Office, for furnishing details on the implementation of the National Historic Preservation Act; Mr. and Mrs. Jim Tindal, for supplying information on the bridge building exploits of Otis Hamer; Maxine Banks, research analyst, and Dwight Smith, sociologist, Environmental Section of the Oregon Department of Transportation for their helpful review of the manuscript and for their moral support of the entire project; to Sheryl Cockrell for her artful pencil sketches of bridges illustrating this volume and for typing drafts of the manuscripts; and to Barbara Cockrell for typing the final manuscript.

Additionally, we extend our thanks to institution staffs who assisted in locating photographs and other historical material on covered bridges: the Oregon Historical Society, the University of Oregon Special Collections, the Lane County Pioneer Museum, the Salem Public Library, and the Washington County Museum.

Finally, we wish to express our appreciation to our wives and families who shared stale sandwiches on trips while searching for covered bridges, who somehow managed to maintain the semblance of a household despite livingrooms scattered with maps and bathtubs filled with washing photographs. For this, we give our heart-filled thanks.

Front cover: North Fork Yachats Bridge.
Back cover: Former Olivant Bridge, Douglas County.
Photo courtesy Oregon Highway Commission.

CONTENTS

Foreword

In an era of modern technology, a covered bridge offers a respite from the hustle and confusion of daily activity. Most of Oregon's covered bridges are nestled on by-ways that could lead to a "make believe world." Covered bridges signify more than a quaint link with the past. They represent the pioneer spirit that sought to settle the west, taming rivers and clearing forests. To the economist, they recall the historical economic trends which were conducive to the movement of goods and people into western Oregon. To the engineer, the covered bridge represents the utilization of native materials in ingenious ways that were perhaps more daring and beautiful than any other place in the United States. To the historian, they connote the story of the people and places for whom the bridges were named, their successes and failures and the passing of a lifestyle which represents man's conquest of his environment. To the artist and photographer, the covered spans are a visual link to the past in which the pastoral setting almost brings back the blare of klaxon horns of vintage automobiles. And to the "student of covered bridges," they conjure visions of a life of solitude and accomplishment, of freshly plowed fields and Sunday afternoon drives on country roads.

It is no wonder, then, that the renaissance of interest in covered bridges should occur as many of these beautiful spans are being bypassed, leaving them standing like sentinels from another time.

This book, a guide to each of Oregon's covered bridges, includes maps, facts and folklore to give the reader and covered bridge enthusiast a broader understanding of the important roles that bridges have played in the settlement of Oregon and the west.

Each of the bridges is cataloged, with data on the date of construction, length, truss type and other salient features. A map is provided, as are written directions to each bridge, with the hope that more individuals can enjoy the serenity of these covered spans before they are lost to "progress."

Please join us in advocating the preservation of the remaining noble structures which serve to remind us of Oregon's determination to preserve the environment and create a better place to enjoy life.

"The old bridge that we knew and loved invited our inspiring artists more than any other point around town. We were proud of it as an engineering feat. Then it had fascinations of its own. It stood in the frontier, dividing our cozy little town from the wilds. The woods on the further side were unspoiled, and a regular jungle grew near the banks downstream, where we went blackberrying. I cannot think of the old bridge without smelling its dusty, stable odors. You remember the rods of light that shot through from the knot holes, and the thump of hoofs and rattle of wheels on the planks. We boys used to plunk stones though the cracks in the flooring into those green swirls below. Anyhow, it was a great old bridge, and no artist could do it justice." (March, 1938)

Extract of a letter from Herbert Thompson, a native of Eugene, referring to the Ferry Street Bridge, built in 1876. Courtesy of the Lane County Pioneer Museum.
Drawing: Old McKenzie River Bridge

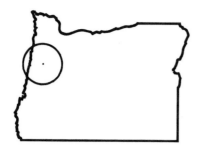

BENTON County

The November 16, 1912 commissioners meeting reviewed the construction costs involved in building the Alsea River covered span near the D. R. Tom residence in the upper Alsea Valley. The bridge had a length spanning 75 feet with an additional 86 feet in approaches. George W. Smith, a county commissioner, detailed the costs:

Gravel	79.00 to Mr. Bailey
Chords	73.00 to D. R. Tom
Freight	106.35
Steel	171.22 to J. T. Phillips, blacksmith
Concrete piers	193.75 to W. E. Earnest
Freight bill	19.25
Cement	138.75 to C. H. Carter
Paint	25.50
Nails	14.25
Freight on cement	30.00
Timber for approach	30.00
Labor	400.00 to W. E. Earnest
Lumber	290.08 to Alsea Lumber Mill
Cast washers	2.70 to J. T. Phillips
5½ bbls cement	15.95
	1,589.80 total costs

Benton County, named for Thomas H. Benton of Missouri, was created and organized December 23, 1847. Corvallis, originally called Marysville by its founder, J. C. Avery, became the first county seat, and was incorporated January 28, 1857. The county boundaries during this period of time included most of what today is Lincoln County as well as its present land area. Towns developing in the 1850s included Monroe, Philomath, "Alseya," Oysterville, Newton, Tidewater, and Yaquina. As communities developed, routes more direct than river travel were needed. Several of the earlier major routes of travel were privately-owned toll roads. Users of these roads complained bitterly of excessive toll charges and asked the county for public control of the toll rates. Benton County entered into an agreement with the Yaquina Bay Wagon Road Company on December 5, 1867 to allow all portions ". . . of the wagon road lying east from a point where said road intersects the county road leading from Corvallis to Kings Valley by way of Matzer's Mill to be open to public travel without toll charge." Dozens of requests for public roads also were filed with the court prior to 1900. The construction costs of roads and bridges became a major portion of the early county budgets.

Early bridge builders in Benton County included H. W. Fiedler, St. John and Stone, A. L. Porter, and Black & Frary. Prior to the arrival of the automobile, construction costs of individual bridges seldom exceeded a few hundred dollars. On October 7, 1885, bids were reviewed for the construction of the Frantz Mill covered bridge over the Luckiamute River. A summary of the bids showed:

St. John & Stone	$474
Jos. Black & Frary	$470
A. L. Porter	$535

The county court awarded the contract to Black & Frary, the low bidder.

Bidding on two Mary's River bridges was closed on April 9, 1920, and on May 5, 1920, the contract to build both bridges was awarded to H. W. Fiedler. Fiedler had agreed to build the covered spans at a contracted price of $1965 each. The Honey Grove bridge contract had been awarded to Fiedler in 1914 for just $498. The uncovered span, just one mile east of Alsea was covered just one year later at a cost of $1188.56, and lasted until the 1960s.

Covered bridges were built in quantities spanning Mary's River, Luckiamute River, and Alsea River, as well as nearly every creek and slough. By 1920, the majority of bridges were covered spans, and during the December 23, 1921 commissioners meeting, the court ordered that Charles Durrell, bridge superintendent, number and keep an inventory of all county bridges.

After 1940, the number of covered bridges in Benton County declined drastically, and by 1955, a dozen covered spans crossed streams in the county. The dismantling of the Moody roofed bridge was noted in 1958. The removal of the Luckiamute River structure between Hoskins and Highway 223 in the Kings Valley area left just ten covered bridges in the county. Ten years later, the number had dropped to three. Gone are such covered bridges as the Kiger Island Bridge, a 340 foot structure; the Dodge Slough Bridge, a small plank-floored building; and the state-owned Kings Valley Bridge, one of the last in the state system. Replaced, too, were the Wren Bridge, a sister of the Harris Bridge; the Bundy Bridge, once a part of a county park; and the Philomath Bridge, saved only temporarily by efforts of a local social club.

Soon, another of the Benton County wooden bridges will be replaced as the Irish Bend Bridge will be removed for the sake of safety and progress. Every effort will be made to utilize the bridge for public enjoyment.

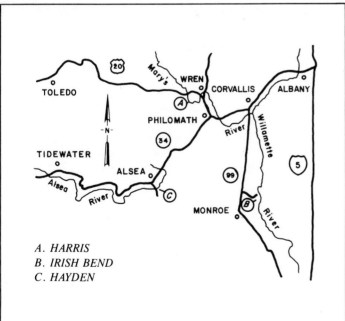

A. HARRIS
B. IRISH BEND
C. HAYDEN

The Kiger Island Bridge. *One of the longer bridge spans in Benton County crossed the Willamette Slough from Corvallis to Kiger Island. In 1914, a proposal was made to house the entire structure, at a total cost of $791.16. Just seven years later, the county restricted the speed of traffic on the bridge to 10 mph, and the structure was load-limited to 14,000 pounds. The old Kiger Island covered span was removed in 1934. A new bridge was designed by State Highway engineers conforming to the specifications for bridges of the Oregon State Highway Commission. The new Kiger Island bridge measured 340 feet in length. Both the top and bottom chords consisted of three 12 x 14 inch timbers side by side. The width of the roadway measured 19 feet, but the vertical clearance was limited to 15 feet, 9 inches. At the time of its replacement in August 1963, the Kiger Island Bridge was Oregon's longest covered span. But, its small portals limited the sizes of loads of farm products.*

Photo: Salem Public Library, Ben Maxwell Collection

HARRIS BRIDGE

Stream: Marys River
Built: 1936
World Guide No.: 37-02-04
T11S R6W S30
Truss: Howe
Length: 75 feet

The Harris Bridge is located on graveled Harris Road just 2½ miles west of Wren, spanning Marys River near the seldom used railroad.

Completed in 1936, the bridge was a replacement of a covered bridge built by H. W. Fiedler. The Harris Bridge retains its rounded portal design, and it wooden plank flooring. Features include wooden piers and narrow slit windows just below the roof line to light the bridge interior. The siding is board and batten style, and the roof is shingled.

Harris has been a community since 1890, bearing the name of a pioneer land owner. When the post office was established, residents petitioned for the name of Harris, but postal authorities feared confusion might develop with near-by Harrisburg. The town was known as Elam, for Mrs. Gladys Elam, the community's first postmaster, and the name was later changed to Harris.

To get there: Take Highway 20 from Corvallis to Wren; then take Harris Road west approximately 2½ miles to the bridge.

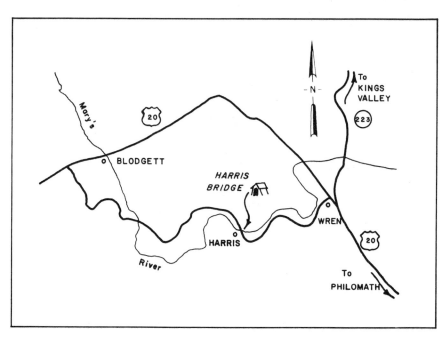

HAYDEN BRIDGE

Stream: Alsea River
Built: 1918
World Guide No.: 37-02-05
T14S R8W S2
Truss: Howe
Length: 91 feet

Spanning Alsea River just two miles west of Alsea, the Hayden Bridge is one of the oldest in the state. Its portals, once rounded in design, have been enlarged to a more modern design to facilitate larger loads. The exterior siding is of vertical board and battens which flares out at the base. A daylighting strip exists below the roof line of both sides of the bridge. The bridge atmosphere is enhanced by a wooden-deck floor.

Alsea was a river community as early as 1850, known as Alseya Settlement. The name is derived from the name of an Indian tribe living at the mouth of the river, originally pronounced in three syllables.

During the heyday of covered bridge construction, several of the covered structures were built closeby on the Alsea River and on the North Fork of the Alsea River. Oregon's last covered span on a primary State Highway, the Mill Creek Bridge on Oregon Highway 34, stood just two miles away. Only the Hayden Bridge stands today.

To get there: From Corvallis, take Oregon Highway 34 to Alsea and continue west on Ore. 34 two miles to Hayden Road. Turn left onto Hayden Road and continue for ¼ mile to the bridge.

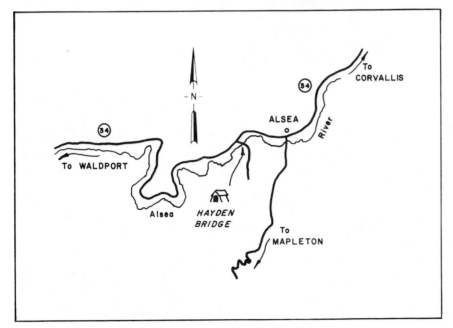

IRISH BEND BRIDGE

Stream: Willamette Slough
Built: 1954
World Guide No.: 37-02-09
T14S R4W S7
Truss: Howe
Length: 60 feet

For Sale: A Covered Bridge

The unique dilemma facing Benton County officials involves disposal of the Irish Bend Bridge, located approximately 6 miles northeast of Monroe. The bridge has been replaced by two large culverts, and is no longer open to traffic. Sitting at the end of a rough gravel road over the Willamette River Slough, the 20-foot long approaches to the bridge can no longer support heavy vehicles, and modern farm equipment is too wide to pass through the narrow 15-foot wide portals.

Historical significance of the bridge is limited, as the bridge was built in 1954. Another problem with the bridge is its short length of just 60 feet. Relocating the bridge over larger streams would be expensive as long approaches would need to be installed.

Interested buyers of the bridge have included a land tract developer, a farmer, a restaurant owner, and Oregon State University. The county hopes it can be put back into service within the county, otherwise it might end up as scrap lumber.

Early Irish settlers in the 1860s gave the name to the area surrounding the bottom land and bend in the Willamette River.

To get there: From Corvallis, travel approximately 12 miles south on Highway 99W. Look for the sign pointing to Irish Bend Road. Turn left and travel 1¾ miles on the paved road. Turn left at the gravel road and continue for 1½ miles to the bridge.

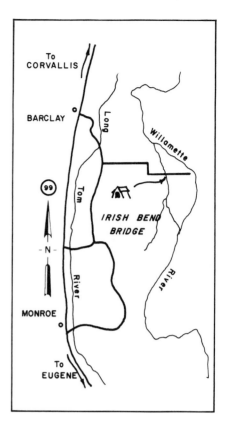

The Hoskins Bridges (Benton County). *The construction of adjacent covered bridges—one for trains and the other for automobiles—was a rarity in Oregon bridge building. These wooden spans across the Luckiamute River, near the site of old Fort Hoskins, survived together until the county bridge was removed in the fall of 1956. The rail span, built by the Valley and Siletz Railroad, featured individually housed trusses. It was replaced in the early 1960's. Such economic construction allowed the truss members to be covered without the potential liability of roof fires. The highway bridge, built in 1932, had the flared sides, white-painted batten siding, and rounded portals typical of Benton County spans.*

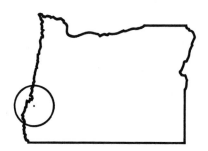

COOS County

Coos County was organized on December 22, 1853, out of portions of Umpqua (later called Douglas) and Jackson Counties. The name Umpqua was derived from Indians inhabiting the region.

In the early periods of settlement, transportation of people and goods was handled primarily by boats along the coast and up the inland waterways. Few miles of wagon road existed in the county in 1872 when J. H. Nosler, early pioneer, gave the Fourth of July oration at Coquille. To the 200 persons present, Nosler ventured the prediction ". . . that the time was not far distant when wagons and buggies would be used in Coos County, and roads built to carry them." It is stated that his audience considered such talk "worse than nonsense."

The process of clearing and settling interior areas of the county progressed slowly. For years the easiest way to reach Coos Bay by land was south from the mouth of the Umpqua River. A trail led along the beach and for many decades this was the only way of connecting the two points by land. Monuments were erected to guide travelers and "prevent accidents from quicksand." It was not until the 1920s that a surfaced road was built approaching Coos Bay from the north, taking traffic away from the beach.

Roads were built linking interior settlements, and covered bridges followed consequentially. John B. Fox was the champion builder of Coos County covered and open spans. Fox arrived in Coos County during the mid-1860s and contracted to build a wharf at Marshfield (now called Coos Bay) about 1868. During the following thirty years, he established himself as a bridge carpenter, road builder, installer of water works and mechanical genius. Fox devised a system of boring holes through logs which he used to install water systems for Marshfield in 1869 (and the second system in 1892) and for Coquille City in 1888.

Fox's talents came to light in bridge construction. He contracted to build bridges across the North Fork of the Coquille River at Burton Prairie in 1881, and at Lee in 1884. His other spans included a crossing over the East Fork of the Coquille at Maynard's Mill in 1887, a bridge at Gravelford about 1883, and a covered crossing at Fairview in 1894. The height of his career as a bridge builder was 1895 when he built or repaired 18 bridges in Coos County.

Residents in the county were cognizant of the importance of bridges. A tiny community near the upper reaches of the Coquille River called Enchanted Prairie was renamed Angora when the townsite was moved closer to the river in the 1880s. A covered span which was constructed at this site in 1894 was referred to as "the Bridge" and the community adopted "Bridge" as its new name. A new covered span was built at Bridge in 1928 and although it had been bypassed in the early 1960s, it survived until 1969 when weight from an abnormally heavy snowfall crushed the roof of the span and the bridge was removed.

Although Coos County now has just one covered bridge, at one time most of the covered railroad bridges in Oregon were located there. In the early 1960s six covered railroad spans were still in use in the county and the Salmon Creek Bridge at Powers had been converted from rail use to accommodate log trucks.

The railroad bridges had been built in 1923 by Southern Pacific to serve the Smith-Powers Logging Company line between Coquille and Powers. Flood waters seriously damaged several of these structures in 1964. All were replaced shortly thereafter.

The Salmon Creek covered bridge at Powers was also built in 1923 to handle rail traffic. When logging activities in the area declined, the bridge was converted to truck use. It was declared unsafe for traffic in the mid-1960s, and at the age of 53 was dismantled.

Most of the county's covered spans were replaced by the 1950s. Several, such as the Lusk Bridge and the Gravelford Bridge succumbed to fires which burned out of control in the Coast Range. Housed spans erected by the State Highway Department fared somewhat better, but only the Sandy Creek Bridge remains intact.

SANDY CREEK (REMOTE) BRIDGE

Stream: Sandy Creek
Built: 1921
World Guide No.: 37-06-09
T29S R10W S33
Length: 60 feet
Truss: Howe

The Sandy Creek covered bridge carried traffic on Oregon Highway 42 until it was by-passed in 1949. This bridge is considered short in comparison to other covered bridges on Oregon highways. The 60-foot span is strengthened by two crossed Howe truss members on each chord, a rarity in short covered trusses. An additional interesting aspect of the bridge is the use of large-framed windows on both sides of the structure, maximizing the illumination of the bridge interior.

The bridge is in relatively poor condition. Both approaches have been removed, and virtually no maintenance has been performed since the span was by-passed. Portal boarding is missing, roof supports are cracked and the roof is in need of repair.

The community of Remote received its name, it is believed, because of its isolation.

To get there: Travel east of Roseburg, 31 miles on Highway 42 to Remote. The Sandy Creek covered bridge is located a stone's throw north of the concrete bridge which replaced it.

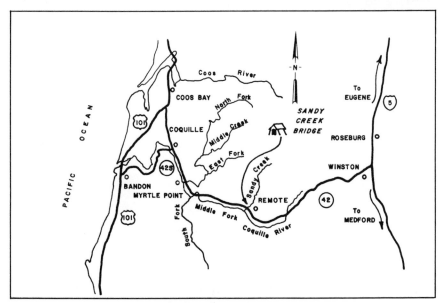

Opposite: The Fox Bridge. In 1872 John B. Fox settled on the North Fork of the Coquille River near the site of a bridge which now bears his name. In exchange for the homesteaded land, Fox paid $10 and a used army pistol. The original Fox Bridge was constructed in 1883 by J. D. Bennett, a local carpenter. Like other county bridges, it employed a Smith truss design which was widely used in southern Oregon prior to World War I. The Fox Bridge was a lofty structure, and featured two windows for increased visibility. The bridge was the victim of a fire in the early 1950's which also burned the tiny Lee Valley Church near the community of Norway. The remains of the wooden bridge were dismantled in 1954. A modern concrete span at the site bears the name of the former bridge.
Photo: Maxwell Collection, Salem Public Library

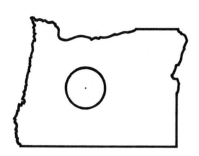

DESCHUTES County

A covered bridge seems totally out of place in the arid climate of central Oregon. The reason for constructing a cover for a wooden bridge in a dry climate is dubious at best. However, county courts which financed such construction, fully believed this was the best way to protect the taxpayer's investment.

The first covered spans east of the Cascades were probably built in Union County, where A. S. Miller built crossings over the Grande Ronde River at Oro Dell and Summerville in 1880. A year later these spans were housed.

Another covered span in a dry climate was located 4 miles northwest of Mitchell, in Grant County. As the county receives as much moisture annually from snow as from rain, it appears that bridge designers covered the structure not by necessity, but by habit. Built in 1917 for $6,774, the span was replaced in 1952 after 35 years of service.

Prior to the construction of the Swalley Canal Bridge in Deschutes County, the Woodsworth Bridge in Hood River County held the distinction of being the last covered bridge built in Oregon east of the Cascades. The Woodsworth Bridge was constructed in the 1920s over the East Fork of Hood River and was located only 12 miles from the snowy slopes of Mt. Hood. High water cracked the truss and the bridge was removed after it was by-passed in 1957.

There is no long standing tradition of building covered spans in central or eastern Oregon. County courts appeared to consider the cost of covering a wooden bridge as an unnecessary extravagance. Thus, the remaining roofed span east of the Cascades was constructed by a man who wished to preserve the nostalgic sentiment of covered bridges.

The Mitchell Bridge. This covered span near Mitchell was one of the few such bridges built east of the the Cascades. In 1917, the structure was jointly built by Wheeler County and the State Highway Department. Since the climate in this region is arid, there appears to be little reason for a covered span. The fact that it was housed was undoubtedly due to the Oregon Highway Department's trend of covering wooden structures built during World War I.
Photo: Oregon State Highway Commission

ROCK O' THE RANGE BRIDGE

Stream: Swalley Canal
Built: 1963 (private)
World Guide No.: 37-09-01
T17S R12E S9
Truss: Modified Kingpost
Length: 42 feet

The Rock O' the Range Bridge is the only Oregon covered span located east of the Cascade Range and is one of the more recent covered bridges to be built in the state. Interestingly, it represents an architectural style of bridges unique to Oregon.

William Bowers was developing a parcel of land north of Bend and needed to build an access road across Swalley Canal to his property. He was inspired by Lane County's Goodpasture Bridge and decided that his bridge should be covered. Bowers instructed Maurice Olson, a local contractor, to construct the bridge according to a picture of a covered bridge found on a calendar.

Specially ordered Douglas Fir timbers were placed upon concrete pilings to support both the dead weight of the bridge and the live load of passing traffic. Although small timbers were added to help strengthen the span, technically a truss arrangement is not used. Cedar siding, shingle roof and side windows were added refinements. The bridge was competed in 1963 for about $4,500.

Bowers has dedicated the bridge to the public. Maintenance costs for the bridge will be borne by landowners who use the bridge for access to their property.

Unlike bridges over a large stream, the Rock O' the Range Bridge is actually built lower than the connecting roadway since the flow of the irrigation canal it crosses poses no hazard to the safety of the structure.

To get there: Travel north of Bend on Highway 97 toward Redmond. The bridge is located two miles north on Bend on Bowery Lane west of the highway.

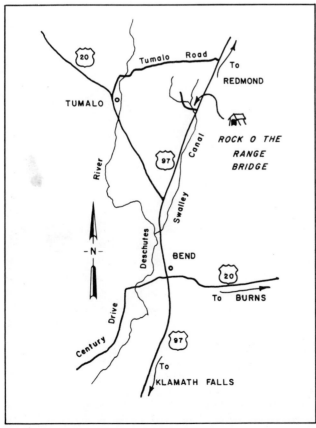

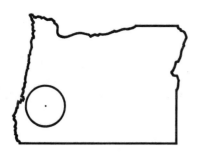

DOUGLAS County

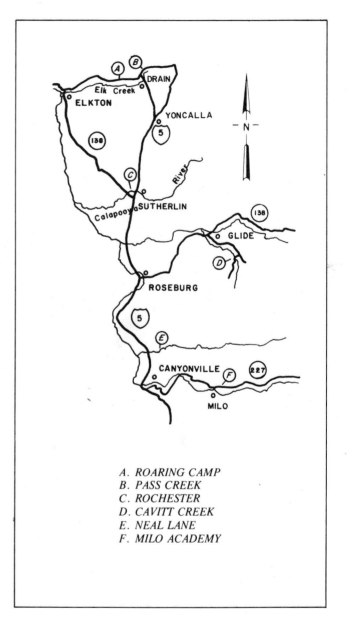

A. ROARING CAMP
B. PASS CREEK
C. ROCHESTER
D. CAVITT CREEK
E. NEAL LANE
F. MILO ACADEMY

The influx of settlers began the organization of Douglas County prior to the 1850s and in 1851, the territorial legislature created Umpqua County, taking the name from a tribe of local Indians. One year later, Douglas County was created out of the eastern part of Umpqua County. Another part of Umpqua County went to create Coos County in 1853, and the remainder of Umpqua County went to Douglas County in 1862. The county was named for Stephen A. Douglas, who was the Democratic candidate for the presidency in 1860. Mr. Douglas had strongly supported Oregon to statehood in the 1850s.

Douglas County lay on the north-south route leading to the Applegate Trail. Portions of this major route became part of the Pacific Highway system after the turn of the century. Bridges of that system were designed and financed by the Oregon State Highway Commission. Perhaps the best known bridges of the Pacific system were the two South Umpqua River bridges near Dillard, constructed in 1918. These bridges were built of wood primarily because of the steel shortage caused by World War I. Each of the Dillard covered bridges cost just over $21,000 to construct and included many features that covered bridges in the state primary and secondary roads soon adopted. Covered spans were built in the early 1920s on Highway 42, known earlier as the Coos Bay-Roseburg Highway. These bridges included the Lower Tenmile, the Looking Glass, and the Big Creek covered bridges and were designed and built according to plans furnished by the Highway Commission, costing about $8,000 each. The cost of these bridges was shared between Douglas County and the State of Oregon. Standard features of the 105-foot bridges included rounded portals, white washed interiors, daylighting with side windows, and laminated flooring. As traffic volume and speed increased, these roofed spans were replaced with concrete structures.

A pair of covered spans on Highway 38 were also built following State Highway Commission plans. One of these, the Mill Creek Bridge was built in 1925 over the small tributary of the South Umpqua River near Scottsburg. The 120-foot span lasted 27 years, finally outliving its useful life in 1952.

One of the notable designers of the Douglas County covered bridges was Floyd C. Frear, long-time county engineer. Frear was instrumental in designing such spans as the Yokum, The North Fork of the Smith River, Cavitt Creek, and the Rochester covered bridges. These spans differed from the standard highway designs in window treatments, portal shapes, and floor construction. Often truss configurations differed, as some county spans included kingpost and queenpost truss designs. A pair of queenpost spans were built across the Calapooya in 1904 near Sutherlin. These two bridges, as well as other county bridges such as the Barton Park and the McDonald covered structures, were destroyed by the fast-paced traffic of the 1960s. The Barton Park Bridge was burned on January 5, 1968 and the McDonald covered bridge, built in 1932, lasted until 1970, spending its last year with the vital trusses uncovered. Another of the Douglas County covered spans, the Quines Creek Bridge over Cow Creek, was a 100-foot structure built in 1913 and lasted until 1958, when the bridge caved in.

The Lone Rock Bridge. *Several state-designed covered spans were constructed in Douglas County subsequent to the steel shortages caused by the demands of World War I.*

The Lone Rock Bridge, spanning the North Umpqua River at Glide, featured improvements designed by state engineers including laminated flooring, larger portal openings, daylighting windows, whitewashed interiors, and concrete piers. The North Umpqua River structure was built in 1922, replacing a river ferry. Construction was supervised by Elmer Metzger, Douglas County engineer. A unique ribbon cutting ceremony transpired during the opening of the bridge. The local judge selected to cut the ribbon and to cross the bridge first was late in arriving for the ceremony, so Indian Mace (Meshe), last chief of the Umpquas, was allowed to ride his horse across the structure before the actual ribbon cutting celebration. In 1959, the destruction of the bridge was supervised by Elmer Metzger, the same person who had supervised the construction 37 years earlier.

Photo: Salem Public Library, Ben Maxwell Collection

PASS CREEK BRIDGE

Stream: Pass Creek
Built: 1925
World Guide No.: 37-10-02
T22S R5W S17
Truss: Howe
Length: 61 feet

The bridge at Drain is one of the few Oregon covered bridges within city boundaries. The structure spans Pass Creek near the junction of Elk Creek, and allows school children to walk each day over its planking to classes. The bridge is faced with vertical 1″ by 12″ boards, and has a shingled roof. The portal trim and fence railing are painted white. The fencing runs through the interior of the bridge and offers a contrast to the brown paint of the bridge.

A snowstorm in 1969 damaged the roof extensively. Work crews stripped the roof and rafters from the structure and rebuilt that portion of the bridge.

The bridge sits parallel to a railroad bridge and adjacent to the school baseball field. The old houses nearby beautifully add to the atmosphere of yesterday. A nearby park has picnicking and restroom facilities.

The town was named for Charles Drain who bought a donation land claim from Jesse Applegate about 1850. Pass Creek flows into Elk Creek, which flows into the Umpqua. The Pass Creek Post Office was established in 1867 but lasted only two years, yielding to the one at Yoncalla in 1869.

To get there: At Drain, travel south toward the school on First Street. The bridge is just north of the school.

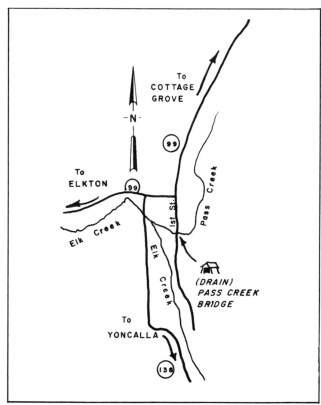

ROCHESTER BRIDGE
Stream: Calapooya River
Built: 1933
World Guide No.: 37-10-04
T25S R6W S13
Truss: Howe
Length: 80 feet

The Rochester covered bridge, with its droopy-eyed appearance, sits just three miles northwest of Sutherlin among the farms surrounding the Calapooya River. The design of this bridge is unique among Oregon roofed structures, featuring windows having graceful curved tops. Built by veteran builder, Floyd Frear, the bridge combines both beauty and strength offered by the wooden structures.

The Rochester structure was remodeled in 1969, when county crews worked to replace portal boarding, the approaches, and the abutments.

The Calapooya River should not be confused with the Oregon Calapooia River in Linn County which supports its own covered bridge at Crawfordsville. The name Calapooya comes from the "Kalpooian" family of Indians which inhabited areas in several counties.

To get there: At Sutherlin, take Highway 138 west approximately 2 miles, then turn north on County Road 10-A and continue for one mile to the bridge.

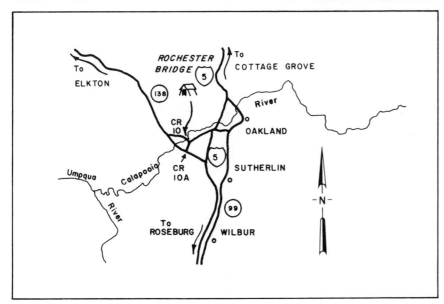

19

CAVITT CREEK BRIDGE

Stream: Little River
Built: 1943
World Guide No.: 37-10-06
T27S R3W S2
Truss: Howe
Length: 70 feet

The Cavitt Creek Bridge, crossing Little River at the junction of Cavitt Creek, is another of the wooden structures built by Floyd C. Frear, noted Douglas County builder. The design features odd-shaped portals to accommodate heavy log truck usage, and the upper and lower chords utilize raw logs as its members. Each side of the roofed structure sports three windows, and long narrow slits above each truss allow "daylighting" as well as ventilation for the bridge interior. The bridge has a metal roof and a floor layered with asphalt. The covered structure sits on concrete piers.

The area surrounding the bridge site was settled in the early 1880s when Abraham Engels, Robert McKure, Robert Cavitt, Emile Shivigny, and others took up donation land grants. The creek and bridge were named for Robert Cavitt, a bachelor who settled on a tributary of Little River.

To get there: From Roseburg, take Highway 138 east to Glide; then take County Road 17A south approximately one mile. Stay left on County Road 17 approximately four miles to Peel. The bridge is approximately one mile past Peel at the intersection of County Roads 17 and 82A.

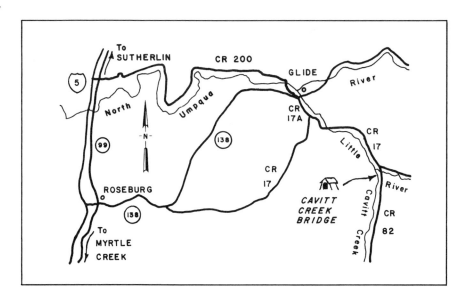

NEAL LANE BRIDGE
Stream: Myrtle Creek
Built: 1929
World Guide No.: 37-10-07
T29S R5W S27
Truss: Kingpost
Length: 42 feet

The Neal Lane Bridge near the town of Myrtle Creek has at least two distinctions; it is one of the shortest covered bridges in Oregon, and the only roofed span in Oregon having a kingpost truss design. The wooden bridge is just 42 feet long, and the addition of the narrow windows make it appear even shorter. Douglas County owns the bridge and is responsible for its maintenance.

The bridge spans Myrtle Creek, a stream used heavily for irrigation. Travellers crossing the bridge will note its cross-wise plank flooring, a single window on either side, a metal roof, and a 5-ton weight limit.

The site at Myrtle Creek, originally settled in 1851, was sold to John Hall in 1862, who established the town in 1865. The name Myrtle Creek was in honor of the nearby groves of Oregon Myrtle, an evergreen tree distinguished by a strong camphor odor.

To get there: At Myrtle Creek, take Main Street east to Riverside Street (County road 18-A) for approximately one mile, turning right onto Neal Lane for another mile to the bridge. Or from Main Street, take County Road 46 (The Myrtle Creek-Days Creek Road) southeast to the intersection with County Road 124. The bridge is at the intersection.

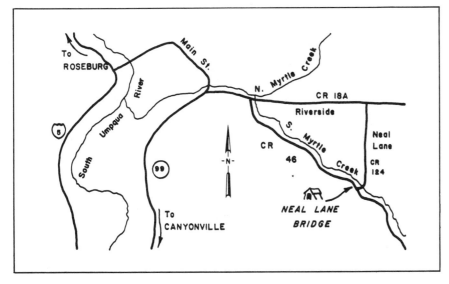

MILO ACADEMY BRIDGE

Stream: South Umpqua River
Built: 1962
World Guide No.: 37-10-10
T30S R3W S26
Truss: Steel
Length: 100 feet

The bridge at the Seventh Day Adventist Academy near Milo is a one-of-a-kind in Oregon covered bridge history. The covering certainly is not a structural necessity, but fills an aesthetic need, as it is Oregon's only steel bridge housed in wood. Since 1920, residents had a covered bridge serving the academy across the South Umpqua River. When the wooden covered bridge was replaced with a steel span, the community felt it had lost a part of its identity. The steel structure was then modified to include the wooden housing, and today, the white-covered bridge stands as a reminder to the residents of their previous covered bridge. The bridge is privately owned and maintained by the Seventh Day Adventist Church.

The area was settled prior to the 1880s, and the post office was established in 1884. Originally known as Perdue, the name was changed to Milo in 1923 when a community member suggested the name of the birthplace of her husband, who was born in Milo, Maine.

A battle is presently boiling over the proposed dam at Day's Creek, which when completed would force backwater upstream inundating the 300-student academy and the covered bridge. Residents have suggested that the Corps of Engineers relocate the dam several miles upstream in the Umpqua National Forest, but a spokesman from the Corps of Engineers said that the Days Creek location offers more benefits with the fewest drawbacks of the 95 different locations investigated. As one resident stated: "It's a shame when physical things like dams become more important than nature and human life."

To get there: At Canyonville, take Highway 227 east past Day's Creek, continue approximately seven more miles to the bridge.

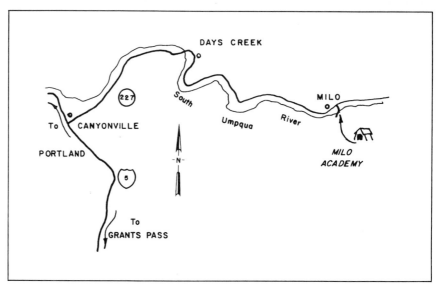

ROARING CAMP BRIDGE
Stream: Elk Creek
Built: 1929
World Guide No.: 37-10-11
T22S R6W S17
Truss: Howe
Length: 88 feet

Nestled among the trees six miles west of Drain just off Highway 38 on a private dirt road, the Roaring Camp Bridge struggles against time, allowing travellers to cross Elk Creek at a slowed pace. The approaches to the unpainted bridge need vertical alignment, so speed must be at a minimum. The bridge, built in 1929, miraculously survived the notorious 1964 flood. Although it lost both approaches, pleas from local residents saved it from destruction.

Features of the old wooden structure include 2″ x 6″ flooring, a cedar shingled roof, and rough-hewn 1″ x 6″ plank siding. Daylighting openings lie just below the roof line almost the entire length of the structure on both sides. The bridge is privately owned and maintained.

Roaring Camp was a road house, located near the bridge. However, an article in the Roseburg News-Review, written by the daughter of Robert Lancaster, builder of the bridge, suggests that the bridge should be called Lancaster Bridge. Some area residents refer to the bridge that way.

To get there: From Drain, take the Drain-Reedsport Highway 38 for approximately six miles. Look for the bridge on the left almost one-eighth mile from the highway.

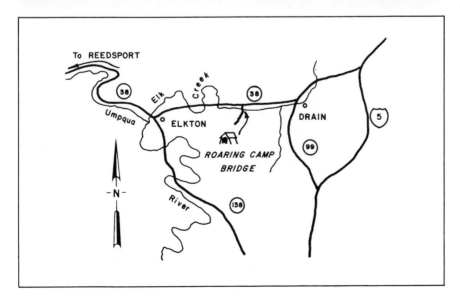

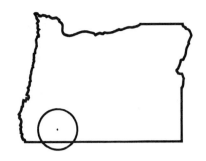

JACKSON County

The southern remoteness of the Jackson County geography allowed the covered bridge builders to alter many of the State Highway Division's bridge design specifications.

Settling of Jackson county began in earnest when gold was discovered in the early 1850s. Towns such as Jacksonville sprang up overnight with adventuresome souls seeking instant wealth. Communities along the Rogue River, Applegate River, and Evans Creek also developed as settlers poured in from the east.

On January 12, 1852, the county was established, obtaining the county name from President Andrew Jackson. Originally much larger, Jackson County was split to form Curry and Josephine Counties. Jacksonville claimed title to the county seat until Medford grew with the railroad, usurping the title.

The Howe truss so widely used throughout the west was virtually unknown in Jackson County. Most bridges constructed in the area were supported by a queenpost truss design or a modification of the queenpost truss. Perhaps, because of expense or because of simplicity in design, the short spans in the county were constructed almost entirely of this truss design. Only the longer McKee covered bridge south of Ruch sports a Howe truss.

Typically, the Jackson County covered bridges exhibit shorter protective portal weather boarding panels, as the area needed to protect is smaller than that of the more common Howe truss. Another feature shared is the flying buttress braces on the outside of the bridge wall, also known as sway braces. These buttress joints had frequent replacement until protective covering of sheet metal was installed to repel the moisture. Shingled roofs remain a distinctive feature, and until the declining years, painting of the covered bridge siding was limited as the expense seemed excessive. Crosswise deck planking has managed to escape the asphalt covering so familiar in other counties. High window slits adding illumination to the bridge interior extend the length of the bridge above the truss tops. Curved portals are popular attractions of the Jackson County design. At first glance, it appears that the builder of the Lost Creek span forgot to complete the job, as there are no end boards to shape a portal.

Covered spans in the county exhibit an average age of 55 years; well past their peak use, and of the two remaining spans still open to traffic, both are semi-retired as the load limits at the Lost Creek and Wimer Bridges are restricted to 8 tons. Since the 1950s, the county has "lost" the Menthorn and Yankee Creek Bridges, and since closed the Antelope and McKee structures to vehicular traffic. The weight restrictions posted on the Yankee Creek covered bridge varied "like a yo-yo," as one bridge user put it. Records showed that the weight limits varied from 2 tons in 1942 to 11 tons in the 1960s. The alternating weight restrictions resulted because of changing conditions of bridge timbers. Repairs on the Yankee Creek roofed bridge began in 1937, which substantially strengthened the structure. Other repairs were made in 1948, 1954, and 1958.

Today, the museum at Jacksonville commemorates the struggles and achievements of those pioneers with historical displays, art, and photographs.

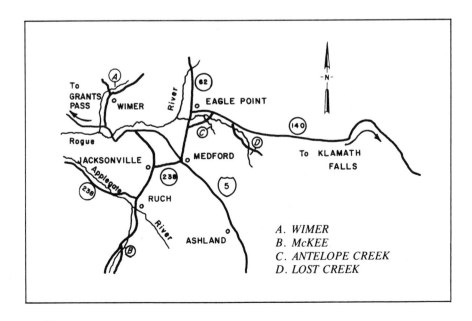

A. WIMER
B. McKEE
C. ANTELOPE CREEK
D. LOST CREEK

The Menthorn Bridge, Jackson County. *The Menthorn Bridge, washed away by the flood waters of the 1964 flood, exhibited most of Jackson County construction features. The covered span was built in 1927, crossing Evans Creek near the town of Rogue River. Features of the 57-foot span included a shingled roof, curved portals, exterior flying buttresses, small portal weather boarding, and a queenpost truss design. Other standard features included vertical boarding, wooden pilings, and narrow daylighting windows above the truss tops.*
Photo: Oregon Highway Commission

ANTELOPE CREEK BRIDGE

Stream: Antelope Creek
Built: 1922
World Guide No.: 37-15-02
T36S R1E S19
Truss: Queenpost
Length: 58 feet

The by-passed Antelope Bridge is struggling against time and nature to remain standing. For years the roofed bridge watched over another covered span just a mile away, spanning Yankee Creek. Before its closure, the Antelope Bridge was restricted to an 11-ton load limit, and the sign remains posted on the portal.

The unpainted siding looks weathered, but the portals are painted white. Roof-line slit windows above the truss tops allow passage of light into the bridge, as does the dilapidated roof. The queenpost truss design is modified by an enclosed kingpost design. Truss members are constructed of 10 x 12s and the plank flooring is constructed of 4 x 12s. The portal protective weather boarding follows the county building pattern of being small in size. Unless the county institutes a plan to maintain this bridge, the future for it appears bleak and short.

To get there: From Medford, travel approximately 5 miles north on Highway 62, then travel east approximately 5 miles to Antelope Road. Travel about 1 mile due south, then turn east and travel another mile to the bridge.

Weathered siding and peeling paint indicate the declining condition of the Antelope Bridge. Traffic using the nearby concrete span keeps constant vigil over the old wooden bridge. The truss design exhibited at the old wooden bridge shows a modification of the usual queenpost style. The enclosed kingpost supporting the queenpost truss adds strength and rigidity to the structural support.

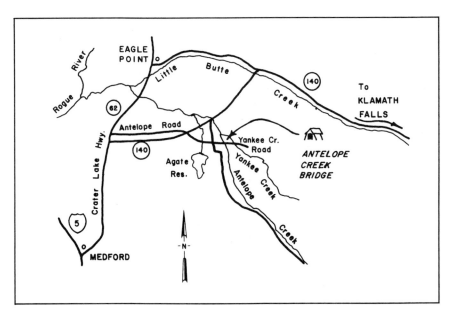

26

LOST CREEK BRIDGE
Stream: Lost Creek
Built: 1919
World Guide No.: 37-15-03
T37S R2E S3
Truss: Queenpost
Length: 39 feet

The Lost Creek Bridge, at 39 feet, is the shortest of all the Oregon covered bridges. The structure is located on a lightly-travelled gravel road, and although still used daily, the bridge has an 8-ton load limit imposed.

Features of the bridge include the usual county queenpost truss design, daylighting by the use of slit windows above the truss tops, a shingle roof, and flying buttress braces. The bridge does not have the usual rounded portal designs at each end, having open ends. The rough, wooden flooring consists of diagonal planking. The hand-hewn truss members are notched and fitted with long bolts through the members, securing them tightly in place.

The bridge was nearly lost in the 1964 Christmas flood. As swirling waters and heavy debris lashed at its piers, residents and concerned bridge enthusiasts prayed during the night that the bridge would be saved. According to a local newspaper, the skies opened and the water receded as morning came. The journalist questioned: Was the bridge saved by prayer?

Many Jackson County residents claim the Lost Creek Bridge to have been built as far back as 1874, making it the oldest covered bridge in Oregon. Historians, however, agree that the bridge was constructed in 1919.

To get there: From Medford, travel approximately 5 miles north on Highway 62, turn east on Highway 140 for about 14 miles to the Lake Creek exit. From Lake Creek, travel 3½ miles on South Fork Little Butte Road to Lost Creek Road. Turn right (south) ½ mile to bridge.

The flooring at the Lost Creek Bridge consists of planking laid in a diagonal pattern. Additional planks lengthwise help to support the weight of passing traffic. The queenpost truss is modified by an "X" within the truss arrangement.

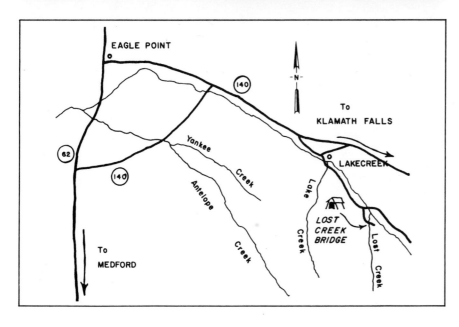

27

WIMER BRIDGE

Stream: Evans Creek
Built: 1927, rebuilt 1962
World Guide No.: 37-15-05
T35S R4W S11
Truss: Queenpost
Length: 85 feet

The Wimer Bridge was saved from destruction when local residents battled to initiate a rebuilding of the weakened structure in 1962. Community members insist that the original bridge was built in 1892, and a sign posted on the bridge claims title to that date. The Hartmans of Jacksonville replaced the Wimer Bridge in 1927.

Features of the Wimer covered span include a shingle roof, the usual daylighting narrow window above the trusses, wooden flooring, and a queenpost truss design. The bridge appears not unlike a barn from downstream, and only the flying buttresses indicate it to be a covered bridge and not a barn over water.

Although rebuilt in 1962, the structure is limited to loads of 8 tons, and no truck traffic is allowed. A service station, the Covered Bridge Restaurant, and a general store are located near the bridge, and during the Bicentennial year, the bridge was used as a sign board to advertise the 4th of July celebration.

Evans Creek was well known as early as 1853 as the site of the Rogue River Indian wars. In the 1880s, the community of Wimer was settled on the banks of Evans Creek. The post office was established in 1886 by members of the Wimer family, residents in the area.

To get there: From Rogue River travel seven miles north on Evans Creek Road to Wimer. The bridge is in the town.

Exterior: The bridge at Wimer spans Evans Creek near the hub of that community's activities. Buttresses outside the bridge wall help to stabilize the bridge against thrusts from wind and vibration from passing traffic.

Interior: Vertical bands of light pass through the cracks between the boards of the exterior siding. The truss design supporting the Wimer Bridge consists of dual queenposts. The smaller truss supports and strengthens the larger one. Traffic is warned of an 8 ton load limit although the bridge was partially rebuilt in 1962.

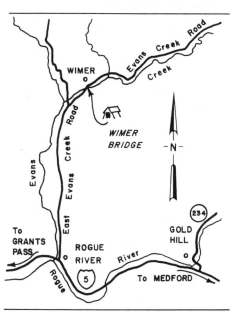

McKEE BRIDGE

Stream: Applegate River
Built 1917
World Guide No.: 37-15-06
T40S R3W S5
Truss: Howe
Length: 122 feet

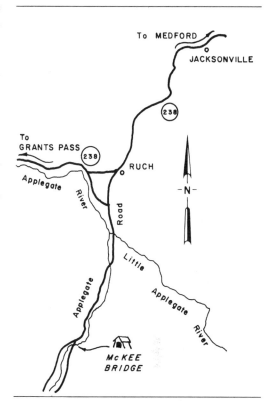

The rustic, well-known covered bridge spanning the Applegate River just eight miles from the California border was built in 1917 by contractor Jason Hartman on land donated by Aldelbert "Deb" McKee. The bridge was used from 1917 to 1956, originally serving the mining and logging traffic.

Lindsay Applegate, for whom the stream is named, prospected the area on the way to the mines in California. The discovery of prosperous mines caused a north-south route to be developed in the area. The covered bridge, being half-way between Jacksonville to the north and the Blue Ledge Copper Mine to the south, was used as a rest stop. Relief horses were kept there for hauling ore from the mine until 1919.

In 1956, the bridge was declared unsafe for vehicular traffic. A sign posted on the end of the bridge hails the combined efforts of the Talisman Lodge, Knights of Phythias, the Upper Applegate Grange, and the Jackson County Court in restoration of the roof in 1965, retaining the structure for pedestrian use. The covered span overlooks a park, and visitors can peer through the five windows on the south side.

Features of the McKee Bridge include a Howe truss design, shortened portal weather boarding, flying buttreesses, open slit windows at the top of each side, and a shingle roof.

To get there: From Medford, travel east on Highway 238 though Jacksonville to Ruch. At Ruch, travel south approximately eight miles on Applegate Road to the bridge site.

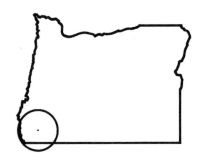

JOSEPHINE County

The Grave Creek Bridge. *When the Grave Creek Bridge was constructed in 1920, State Highway Commission plans for covered bridges called for standard Howe trusses, whitewashed bridge interiors, laminated flooring, strategically placed windows for daylighting, and rounded portals. In later years, larger trucks and busses caused county and state engineers to reconsider the portal shape and size, and most bridge portals reflected the change to a square design. This photograph recorded the Grave Creek Bridge when U.S. 99 was Oregon's major north-south route. In addition, the bridge portals had not yet been reshaped, and cedar shingles still were the covering for the bridge roof. Josephine County's only covered bridge can be visited easily by motorists travelling along Interstate 5 about 15 miles north of Grants Pass.*

Photo: Oregon Historical Society

Much of the history in the 1840-1850s of the area known today as Josephine County was based on the discovery of gold, the search of a southern route leading to the east, and Indian Wars of the 1850s. Early attempts to locate a passable east-west trail in the north had failed, and a southern route was needed. Discovery of the southern route occurred in the 1840s, and in 1846 the Applegate family led the immigrants to the Oregon Territory by the newly explored southern route. The Crowley family was among the 1846 caravan. Their daughter, Martha Leland Crowley, was taken ill and died at the crossing of the stream now called Grave Creek. The caravan party constructed her coffin from a wagon box, and buried her under an oak tree. All traces of her burial were obliterated, and the cattle were corralled over the grave site so the Indians would be unable to find the grave and exhume the body for the garments. Apparently the Indians found the grave, according to a Colonel Nesmith, who visted the area in 1848, as bones were scattered about the pit. He replaced the bones, and refilled the pit with earth.

In 1852, a lesser chief of the Rogue River Indians, known as Taylor, along with several of his braves, murdered seven white men during a cloudburst at Grave Creek. Taylor, not wanting a treaty with the whites, reported finding the men drowned. However, in June 1852, Taylor and three of his warriors were captured by a posse and hanged. A year later, several Indians were killed in a skirmish a few days after the War of 1853, and their bodies were buried in the grave along with Martha Crowley. A historian recorded the event:

> "Miss Crowley's remains rest, perhaps, with those of the savages who desecrated her last abode. . . . Thus from the death and burial of Miss Crowley, Grave Creek obtained its name."

> A. G. Walling, 1884

A man named Bates soon opened a famous place of entertainment for travellers, then sold it to two men, James Twogood and a gentlemen named McDonald Harkness. The 1854 Legislature established the name of the community as Leland Creek to honor Martha Crowley, and the firm of Harkness and Twogood called their place the Leland Creek House. Harkness was killed by Indians in the spring of 1856, and Twogood left the area, going to Boise, Idaho for safety. Later, the name of the establishment was changed to the Grave Creek House. The years have erased the community of Leland, but the name of Grave Creek lives on.

Josephine County was officially established January 22, 1856 from the western side of Jackson County. The county was named for Josephine Rollins, a daughter of a gold miner who discovered the creek.

Although numerous bridges were constructed spanning the Rogue, the Illinois, and the Applegate Rivers, as well as many of the creeks, few were covered. Historical records indicate that covered bridges were constructed on the Applegate River, west of Grants Pass near Highway 199; on the Illinois River, west of Grants Pass near Highway 199; and on Grave Creek, one mile east of Sunny Valley. Only the Grave Creek Bridge stands today.

GRAVE CREEK BRIDGE

Stream: Grave Creek
Built: 1920
World Guide No.: 37-17-01
T34S R6W S11
Truss: Howe
Length: 105 feet

The Grave Creek covered span at Sunny Valley can be seen by motorists from Interstate 5, about 15 miles north of Grants Pass. Features of the wooden structure include a metal roof, six gothic-style windows on either side, concrete abutments, a Howe truss, square portals, and a coat of white paint. The old wooden river crossing is the last covered bridge on the north-south Pacific Highway system.

Existing records on the Grave Creek

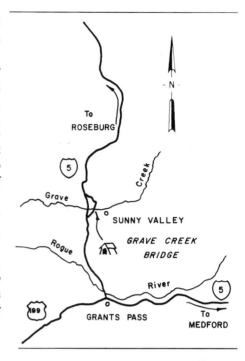

Bridge state that contract number 263 was awarded by the Oregon State Highway Department to J. Elmer Nelson on April 27, 1920. Just four months later, August 31, traffic passed through its portals. A. A. Clausen, resident engineer in Josephine County, was in charge of design and construction. He reported that the 105-foot Howe truss was supported by "dumb bell" concrete piers with 114 feet of timbered frame trestle approach spans. Total cost of the construction, including the engineering fee of $1,722.70, is listed at $21,128.65.

To get there: From Grants Pass, travel 15 miles north on Interstate 5 to the Sunny Valley exit. Travel east on the exit road, then travel north for about 1 mile to the bridge.

31

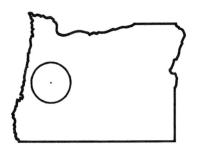

LANE County

When Eugene Skinner founded a small settlement on the banks of the Willamette River in 1847, he probably had little reason to think that "Eugene City" would become one of the major cities in Oregon.

Within several years other pioneers settled in nearby areas and Lane County, named after Governor Joseph Lane, was founded in 1851.

Eugene City was chosen as the county seat in 1853, and by 1880 the population had reached 1,200 people.

By the 1870s the railroads had come to western Oregon, making a terminus near Eugene City. Junction City to the north, lay at the junction of the Oregon Central and the Oregon and California railroads.

One of Lane County's most important bridge constructions was the Eugene City span in 1876 which replaced a ferry operated by Eugene Skinner. The "Ferry Street Bridge" survived the 1890 flood and was replaced 23 years later.

Lane County's dedication to the construction and maintenance of covered bridges began in earnest in the 1870s with A. S. Miller and Sons, who had their offices in Eugene for a number of years. Beginning in 1881, and continuing for the next 20 years, Nels Roney constructed numerous covered bridges in the county. Often Miller and Roney competed against each other for bridge contracts.

County bridge superintendents in the early 1900s wisely advocated the construction of covered structures. Tradition, of course, played a part, but cost was an important consideration. A Eugene *Morning Register* editorial in 1915 reported that the "Lane County court is convinced that wooden bridges properly built will last as long as steel and they know the cost is much less."

Lane County was the first county to build covered bridges on a large scale and the last to discontinue using them. The county built covered structures into the 1940s (Lowell, 1945; Brumbaugh, 1948; Dorena, 1949) and replaced the covered Belknap Bridge, which was washed out in the Christmas Flood of 1964, with another covered span in 1966.

County engineers were quick to use truss and housing designs furnished by the State Highway Department. As a result, Lane County bridges are all similar in design, which included use of the Howe truss, vertical batten siding, "daylight" roofline windows and white painted exteriors.

Because it has such a history of covered bridges, the county is reluctant to replace them, preferring instead to construct a by-pass whenever possible. It seems appropriate that family names such as Brumbaugh, Ernest, Currin, and Goodpasture should be retained in history by these nostalgic structures.

Old timers can name bridges which have long been replaced—Creswell Bridge, Hendricks Bridge, Red Bridge, Sailor's Bridge, Brice Creek Bridge. Fortunately, the majority of covered bridges in the county will remain standing. County commissioners have stated that the county's bridge population will be maintained at least at nineteen, if possible, demonstrating that the trend toward destroying wooden bridges can be reversed.

Unfortunately, the cost of maintaining covered spans has steadily increased, causing the county to reevaluate its commitment to the retention of covered spans. County experience has indicated that a covered bridge requires deck maintenance and structural retuning about every two years, repairs for structural rotting at seven-year intervals, and repairs to the portals every other year. The bridges also require frequent inspection. By 1981, the county expects to complete a capital improvement program to replace or by-pass a number of spans which carry a high level of traffic and which will soon be in need of extensive repairs. Listed for closure to traffic are the Goodpasture, Wendling, Brumbaugh, Currin, Nelson, Coyote, Meadows and Lowell Bridges.

Although the spans are to be removed from the existing road system, county officers are quick to point out that the replacement of covered bridges does not necessarily mean "destruction" for these aesthetic structures.

While many counties did not move to preserve covered bridges until many of the structures had been demolished, the effort to spare the nostalgic structures began in the early 1950s in Lane County. The most destructive force in destroying covered spans since 1960 has been water, not man, as five roofed structures were washed out or severely damaged as a result of the 1964 Christmas flood.

Although a conscious commitment for preservation of bridges has been made, finding someone to perform work on the structures is difficult. Only a few old timers on the county's bridge crew understand the peculiarities of covered spans. "Most bridge men would rather build new covered bridges than work on old ones," said former bridge superintendent Ed Stonecypher. "In the winter they're always drafty and cold, and in the summer they're dusty and hot."

The Ferry Street Bridge. *The Eugene City bridge or "Ferry Street Bridge" was built in 1876 by A. S. Miller at the site of the ferry which had been operated for a number of years by Eugene Skinner, founder of the city of Eugene. In 1890, the northern span and approach was washed away and much of the surrounding countryside inundated. With the bridge left "high and dry," the work to replace the north approach was awarded to L. N. Roney.*

Upon completion, the two spans totaled 350 feet in length. The approaches to the bridge were so steep that drivers of wagon teams had to help push their loads of cargo up into the bridge. Early automobiles also experienced difficulty in overcoming the steepness of the grade. One of Eugene's most beloved landmarks, the bridge was replaced by a steel span in 1913.

Photo: Lane County Pioneer Museum

A. MEADOWS
B. DEADWOOD CREEK
C. LAKE CREEK
D. WILDCAT CREEK
E. COYOTE CREEK
F. ERNEST
G. WENDLING
H. GOODPASTURE
I. BELKNAP
J. HORSE CREEK
K. PENGRA
L. UNITY
M. LOWELL
N. PARVIN
O. CHAMBERS
P. CURRIN
Q. MOSBY CREEK
R. STEWART
S. BRUMBAUGH
T. DORENA
U. OFFICE

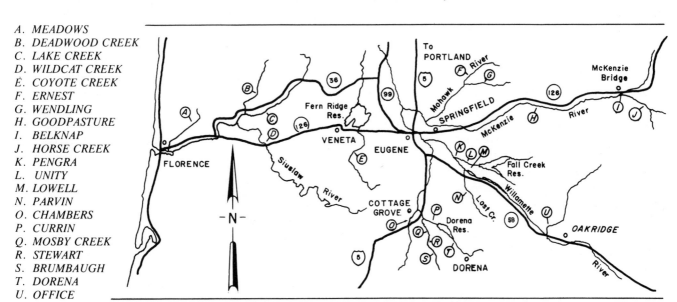

COYOTE CREEK BRIDGE
(Battle Creek Bridge)

Stream: Coyote Creek
Built: 1922
World Guide No.: 37-20-02
T18S R5W S29
Truss: Howe
Length: 60 feet

Coyote Creek Bridge was originally part of Territorial Road and was included in the state secondary road system. Truck traffic became too heavy for the bridge and a more direct highway route was constructed, perhaps insuring a longer life for the covered span.

Heavy snowfall severly damaged the Coyote Creek Bridge in 1969 as the weight of 3½ feet of snow collapsed the entire roof. Chainsaws were used to saw off the rafters and the bridge remained uncovered until early spring when county crews replaced the entire roof.

The few houses near the bridge comprise the community of Hadleyville. Although Hadleyville had a post office in 1890, by 1903 all mail service was conducted through the post office in the village of Crow, two miles to the north.

The Coyote Creek Bridge is often called the Battle Creek Bridge because it is located on Battle Creek Road. Others refer to it as the Swing Log Bridge because it was called that many years ago. Most folks, however, refer to it as the Coyote Creek Bridge.

Design elements include housed buttresses, roofline windows, and square portals. Although it is a short span, for years it has carried a 10-ton weight limit.

To get there: From Eugene, travel 6 miles west on Oregon 126 to Crow Road. Take Crow Road southwest to its intersection with Territorial Highway. Go south 1 mile to Battle Creek Road. Turn west. The bridge is located about 100 yards from the junction.

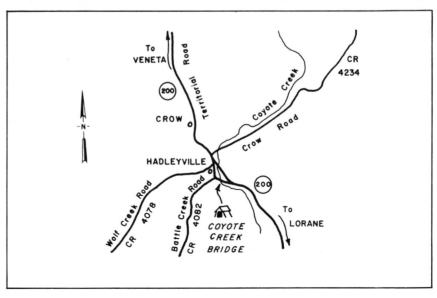

WILDCAT BRIDGE
Stream: Wildcat Creek
Built: 1925
World Guide No.: 37-20-04
T18S R8W S16
Truss: Howe
Length: 75 feet

The Wildcat Bridge is located on a small winding road a short distance from Highway 126 (Route F). From the point where Wildcat Creek flows into the Siuslaw River, Stagecoach Road hugs the hillside until it drops into the narrow plain at Swisshome. Stagecoach Road was the original road to the coast, by-passed in the mid-thirties after the Linslaw Tunnel and Mapleton Bridge were built.

As with many of the bridges built in this area, the Wildcat Bridge boasts of one-piece lower chords which are 16″ x 16″ x 113 feet, the upper chords also of one-piece fir 12″ x 12″ x 47 feet.

The span is closed to trucks and has a posted weight limit of 10 tons. An 18 x 3 foot window on the east side provides a view of oncoming traffic. The roof is covered with corrugated tin. Nearby Austa boat ramp provides access to the river for fishermen on the Siuslaw River.

To get there: Travel 33 miles west of Eugene on Oregon Highway 126. At this intersection, Stagecoach Road connects from the north, with Wolf Creek Road to the south.

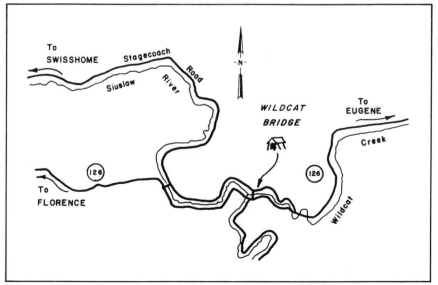

LAKE CREEK BRIDGE
Stream: Lake Creek
Built: 1928
World Guide No.: 37-20-06
T17S R8W S9
Truss: Howe
Length: 105 feet

Some confusion exists as to the name of this bridge. Some prefer to call it the Lake Creek Bridge after the stream it crosses; to some it is the Nelson Creek Bridge, named for the Nelson Mountain Road of which it is a part. Still others dub it the Nelson Bridge, after a small forest service camp in the vicinity many years ago.

The bridge was built in 1928 for the modest price of $3,155. A year later, improvements totalling $183 were made. The single piece chords measure 14″ x 14″ x 111 feet for the lower timbers and 12″ x 12″ x 79 feet for the upper beams.

Portal boards on both ends were recently replaced because they had been broken by the high loads of log trucks.

To get there: Travel north from Mapleton on Highway 36. The Nelson Mountain Road turnout is located near milepost 17. The bridge is situated only ½ mile from the highway on the Nelson Mountain Road.

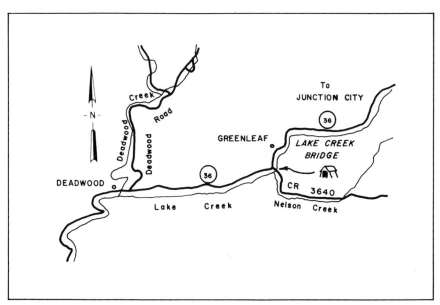

MEADOWS BRIDGE
Stream: North Fork Siuslaw River
Built: 1922
World Guide No.: 37-20-09
T17S R11W S24
Truss: Howe
Length: 105 feet

The Meadows Bridge is a structure which has outlasted the average lifespan of most covered bridges. Now in its sixth decade of service, the span handles a heavy traffic of log trucks and is likely to be replaced or bypassed in the next several years.

The bridge exhibits such architectural refinements as housed buttresses, roofline daylight illumination, and a large window on the east side.

Built to provide access to the residents on McLeod Creek, the Meadows Bridge has reached the point at which extensive repairs must be made if the span is to remain in service. Such repair would probably equal the cost of replacing the structure with a concrete bridge.

To get there: Travel one mile east of Florence on Oregon 126 to the North Fork Road. Follow the road along the North Fork of the Siuslaw River for seven miles to the intersection of the McLeod Creek Road, where the bridge is located.

Alternate route: Travel north from Mapleton on Highway 36 for three miles to Brickerville. Turn left on FS 1706. The road climbs to the McLeod Creek divide and descends to link with the North Fork Road.

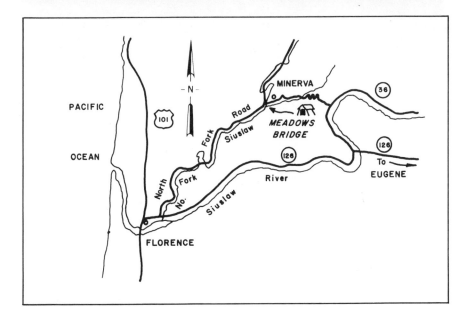

GOODPASTURE BRIDGE

Stream: McKenzie River
Built: 1938-39
World Guide No.: 37-20-10
T16S R2E S29
Truss: Howe
Length: 165 feet

Goodpasture Bridge is one of the most beautiful and most photographed covered bridges in the state. Designed by the State Highway Department and built by Lane County, the classical, timeless architecture of this bridge is accentuated by Gothic style windows on both sides.

Lane County spent $13,154 constructing the Goodpasture Bridge and is still reaping the benefits of a good investment. Unfortunately, both time and traffic are taking their tolls. The bridge is scheduled to be by-passed about 1980.

The nearby town of Vida was once called Gate Creek, resulting in confusion with Gales Creek in Washington County. "Vida" was selected as an alternate name because it was also the name of the daughter of postmaster Francis Peport. The Goodpasture family settled in an area near the town of Vida and gave their name to the bridge.

To get there: Travel east of Springfield on the McKenzie River Highway, 24 miles to the community of Vida. The Goodpasture Bridge is located at the west edge of Vida.

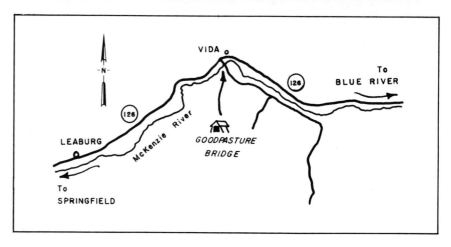

BELKNAP BRIDGE

Stream: McKenzie River
Built: 1966
World Guide No.: 37-20-11
T16S R5E S20
Truss: Howe
Length: 120 feet

Belknap Bridge occupies a site housing a covered bridge since 1890. In that year, the original covered span was erected by Mr. T. Thomson. In 1911, the first bridge was replaced by Lane County with another covered structure. The third covered bridge at this site was erected in 1939 and was destroyed by the Christmas Flood of 1964. The current covered span was designed by the Oregon Bridge Corporation of Springfield and was built by contract let by the county. It was opened for traffic on October 31, 1966, and is the newest covered bridge in the state.

Several years ago louvered gothic windows were added to the south side of the bridge to give interior illumination and to reduce the "box effect" of a windowless span.

To get there: Travel east of Springfield on Highway 126 to the town of McKenzie Bridge. One mile west of the town, turn south onto McKenzie River Drive and continue approximately 1 mile to the bridge.

Lower photo: The third covered bridge to occupy this site was photographed as it was being dismantled in 1939, after 28 years of service. Most covered bridges reach a critical point after 20 years of use and require extensive repairs to maintain the structure in a safe condition.

Photo: Oregon Historical Society

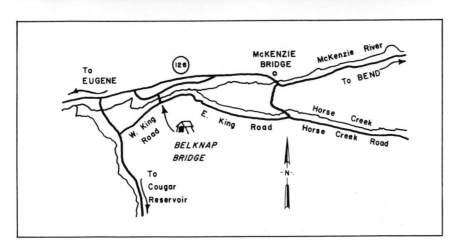

HORSE CREEK BRIDGE

Stream: Horse Creek
Built: 1930
World Guide No.: 37-20-12
T16S R5E S24
Truss: Howe
Length: 105 feet

Horse Creek Bridge exhibits little variation in the basic Howe truss design adopted by Lane County. The 105-foot span was a favored length of county engineers. A window on the west side of the bridge provides extra visibility to the driver of traffic on the curved approach. The bridge is supported by pilings and has a corrugated metal roof.

A. N. Striker constructed a 103-foot Howe covered span in 1904 which was replaced in 1930. The replacement bridge was built for $2,452, with upper chords of 12″ x 12″ x 64 feet and lower chords of 14″ x 14″ x 111 feet.

Horse Creek gained its name in an unusual manner. Historical accounts related that emigrants in the 1850s, succeeded in getting a wagon over the summit of the Cascades near the present McKenzie Pass, and got their wagon a considerable distance down the west side. As they were crossing a stream near the McKenzie River, the horses broke loose and could not be retrieved. Later settlers named the stream Horse Creek after this unfortunate occurrence. In 1968, Horse Creek Bridge was by-passed by a new concrete span and the road received a new alignment. Recently, several young persons requested permission from Lane County to board up the abandoned bridge and live in it. Permission was quickly and strongly denied.

To get there: Travel east of Springfield on U.S. 126 to McKenzie Bridge. Follow Horse Creek Road southeast 1 mile to the bridge.

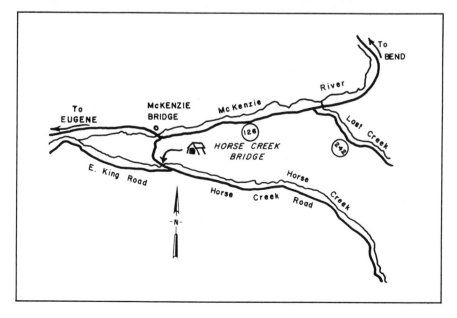

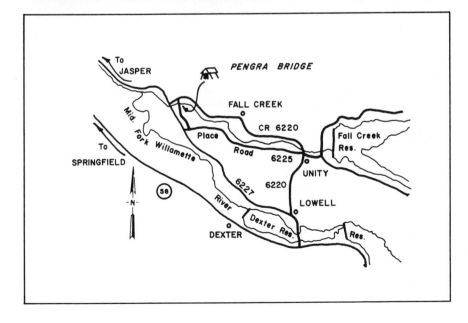

PENGRA BRIDGE

Stream: Fall Creek
Built: 1938
World Guide No.: 37-20-15
T18S R1W S32
Truss: Howe
Length: 120 feet

Pengra Bridge contains two of the longest timbers ever cut for a bridge in Oregon. The timbers for the lower chords, 16″ x 18″ x 126 feet, were cut by the Booth-Kelley Lumber Company east of Springfield. Since 18″ chords were too large to be run through a mill, they were rough-hewn in the woods, transported to the bridge site by truck and resurfaced before being set into place. The dimensions of the upper chords are similar proportions, 14″ x 18″ x 98 feet. The use of one piece chords simplified construction techniques and resulted in a stronger truss, but handling such large timbers was often difficult.

The Pengra Bridge replaced a 192-foot span built in 1904 which had been only a few feet upstream from the present structure.

Pengra was a station on the Cascade Line of the Southern Pacific Railroad and was named for B. J. Pengra, a pioneer of 1853 who became general surveyor of Oregon in 1862. Pengra had surveyed the route of the Oregon Central Military Road to link the Willamette Valley with the Owyhee mining country of eastern Oregon. The road was finished to the summit of the Cascades in 1867, but was seldom used. Later Pengra conceived the idea of building a rail line to Winnemuca, Nevada, and on to Salt Lake City. His survey passed over a considerable portion of the Oregon Central Military Road but the railroad was never built.

The Pengra-Unity Road, once called Pengra Road, lies on an old railroad grade. The road has been renamed Place Road.

To get there: Follow Oregon 22 (Jasper Road) south of Springfield to Jasper and continue travelling southeast on Pengra Road 4 miles to the Little Fall Creek Road. Turn east and travel ¼ mile to Place Road. The bridge is located 100 yards south on Place Road.

UNITY BRIDGE

Stream: Fall Creek
Built: 1936
World Guide No.: 37-20-17
T19S R1W S2
Truss: Howe
Length: 90 feet

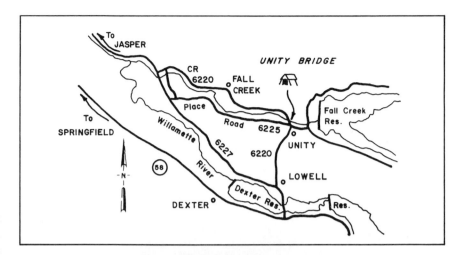

In 1890, the first bridge across Fall Creek was constructed by Nels Roney. That 129-foot Howe truss structure cost Lane County $2,925.50.

A new covered span was built three-fourths of a mile upstream in 1936 at the community of Unity. The county used a standardized 90-foot Howe truss design, but added a full length window on the east side to give motorists a glimpse of oncoming traffic. This adds an aesthetic effect to the structure, also. The county spent only $4,400 in constructing the span.

The original bridge was finally removed in 1953, having served as a foot bridge since 1936.

To get there: Unity Bridge can most easily be reached by traveling north of Lowell for 2 miles to Unity. South of Eugene, follow Oregon 58 to Lowell, then travel north on Lowell to the bridge at Unity.

LOWELL BRIDGE
Stream: Middle Fork Willamette River
Built: 1945
World Guide No.: 37-20-18
T19S R1W S23
Truss: Howe
Length: 165 feet

When Amos Hyland settled on the Middle Fork of the Willamette River in 1874, he plotted a small townsite and named it after his birthplace of Lowell, Maine.

Hyland operated a ferry across the Willamette near the present site of the Lowell Bridge until Nels Roney built the first bridge at Lowell in 1907. Roney was paid $6,295 for the 210-foot Howe span.

In 1915, the entire bridge was raised 5 inches so that rotted wood could be replaced and the original camber be restored.

A truck mishap in the old Lowell Bridge in the early 1940s knocked the truss out of alignment. The Roney-built bridge was replaced at a cost of $25,473 in 1945. Two years later it was housed.

In 1953, the whole bridge was raised 6 feet and the roadway rebuilt in anticipation of the flooding produced by Dexter Dam. The engineers' estimates were correct, and water has never risen closer than 2 feet from the bottom of the bridge.

Some of the heaviest truck traffic in Oregon passes through the Lowell Bridge, transporting logs to the mill in Lowell. It is the heavy load capacity of modern trucks which is literally destroying the bridge. Submerged pilings under the bridge were recently replaced and the roof has developed a discernible sag.

The Lowell Bridge is scheduled to be replaced very shortly. Unfortunately, the bridge cannot be easily bypassed since the road is a straight route.

To get there: From the junction of Interstate 5 and Oregon 58, travel southeast 15 miles to the Lowell Bridge spanning the channel of the Middle Fork of the Willamette River.

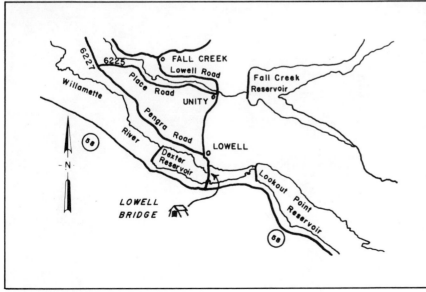

PARVIN BRIDGE

Stream: Lost Creek
Built: 1921
World Guide No.: 37-20-19
T19S R1W S21
Truss: Howe
Length: 75 feet

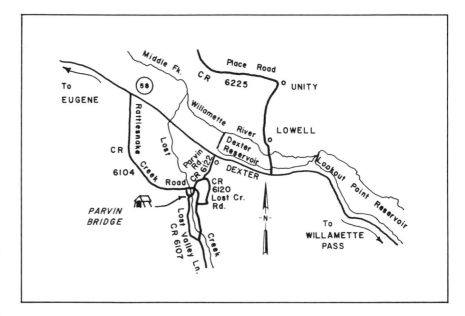

The original bridge at this site was a 66-foot Howe truss span. In an inspection report in 1917 on the structure, bridge inspector J. W. McArthur noted,

"An old bridge. Chords badly worm eaten. Downstream chord has been reinforced in middle by a timber bolted on. Wood is but little better than a powder from worm action. All signs indicate a new bridge in from 2 to 4 years."

Four years later, George W. Breeding erected the present 75-foot Howe span at this location. The cost of the structure was $3,617.82 and included a 62-foot east approach and a 17-foot west approach.

Lost Creek was once referred to as Lost Valley, perhaps because of its remoteness in the 1850s when the first settlers came through the area. The post office at Dexter was established in the early 1870s and was called Butte Disappointment in reference to a local landmark named by pioneers who became lost in the vicinity about 1853. In 1875, the name of the settlement was changed to Dexter because the old name was inconvenient, but no one knows why the name Dexter was selected.

The Parvin Bridge, located on Parvin Road, was named for a pioneer family in the area. The bridge was bypassed when the road was realigned.

To get there: From Dexter, follow Lost Creek Road to Parvin Road. Travel on Parvin Road about 1 mile, crossing Rattlesnake Road, to the covered bridge.

CURRIN BRIDGE

Stream: Row River
Built: 1925
World Guide No.: 37-20-22
T20S R3W S36
Truss: Howe
Length: 105 feet

Nels Roney constructed the first covered bridge at this site in 1883 for $1,935. When it was to be replaced in 1925, the county again considered a contract for the bridge construction. The lowest bid for the structure was $6,520.22, but the county felt it could save money by building the span itself. County employees constructed it for $4,024.88, a savings of $2,495.

As with many Lane County landmarks, the Currin Bridge was named after an early pioneer family in the area. Architectural distinctions include single-piece hand hewn chords, cross-wise planking on the approaches and a corrugated metal roof. It is also the only Lane County covered span with white portals and red sides. Unfortunately, Lane County will by-pass the Currin Bridge in the late 1970s.

To get there: Travel 4 miles east of Cottage Grove on Row River Road to the intersection of Lang Road. The bridge crosses Row River at this intersection. It is located 1 mile from Mosby Creek Bridge, also on Lang Road.

DORENA BRIDGE

Stream: Row River
Built: 1949
World Guide No.: 37-20-23
T21S R2W S24
Truss: Howe
Length: 105 feet

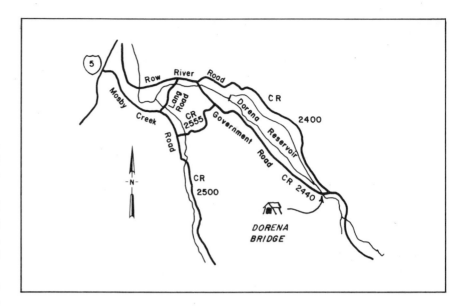

When Dorena Dam was built in 1946, plans were made to build a bridge at the upper end of the reservoir, spanning the Row River.

Government Road along the west bank was completed in 1948 and the Dorena Bridge was built a year later, after the reservoir was filled, at a cost of $16,547.

This bridge is often referred to as the "Star Bridge" because it provided access to the Star Ranch. Once a large and proud estate, the ranch has dwindled to about 100 acres.

The state-designed bridge was bypassed in 1974 by a concrete span. Eventually a park may be built around the bridge site.

Bridge features include spliced chords, daylight roof-line windows and a wooden shingle roof.

The original town site, named for Dora Burnette and Rena Martin (by combining parts of their first names), is underwater at the bottom of Dorena Reservoir.

A railroad in the vicinity served the mining camps until the gold mines played out. The lumber industry de-veloped and used the rails to ship logs to Cottage Grove. The rails still are used for log trains and a steam-powered excursion train.

To get there: Travel 5 miles east of Cottage Grove on Row River Road to the junction of Government Road. The bridge is located on Government Road 7 miles from the junction.

MOSBY CREEK BRIDGE

Stream: Mosby Creek
Built: 1920
World Guide No.: 37-20-27
T21S R3W S1
Truss: Howe
Length: 90 feet

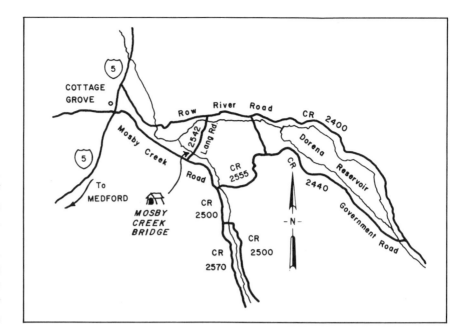

Mosby Creek Bridge is Lane County's oldest bridge, built in 1920, at a cost of $4,125. It is one of the few Lane County bridges supported by wooden pilings instead of concrete abutments.

Spliced chords and steel rod cross braces on the upper chords of the bridge are modifications of the basic Howe truss design. Instead of cedar shingles, the housed span utilizes a corrugated metal roof.

As with most of the covered bridges in the Cottage Grove area, vandals using cans of spray paint have left their mark on the bridge.

The Mosby Creek Bridge is one of three bridges which can be seen from the Oregon, Pacific and Eastern steam excursion train.

The stream was named for David Mosby, a pioneer of 1853 who staked claim to 1,600 acres of land east of the present city of Cottage Grove.

To get there: Leaving Interstate 5 at Cottage Grove, travel southeast on Row River Road approximately 2 miles to the Row River Connection Road. Turn right, cross the railroad, and follow Mosby Creek Road southeast 2 miles to Lang Road. Mosby Creek Bridge is located on Lang Road 2/10ths of a mile from the junction.

STEWART BRIDGE

Stream: Mosby Creek
Built: 1930
World Guide No.: 37-20-28
T21S R3W S1
Truss: Howe
Length: 60 feet

Stewart Bridge is showing the effect of its age. Extensive repairs have been made on the structure in recent years to correct the damage that made the bridge unusable. Heavy rains of the 1964 "Christmas flood" brought water raging down Mosby Creek: the force of the water and the debris it carried cracked the lower chords of the bridge. The snowfall in January 1969 was unequalled in recent history as 3½ feet covered parts of the Willamette Valley. The roof bracing gave under the weight of the snow and the entire roof caved in.

The Stewart Bridge's woes have not stopped. During summer months, the water beneath the bridge is a favorite swimming hole for local youngsters who remove pieces of siding in order to use the bridge as a diving platform. County bridge maintenance crews placed heavy timbers over the truss members to discourage vandalism, but this has not been totally successful. Graffiti-minded individuals, using spray paint, have left indelible marks on the portal boarding.

Nevertheless, the Stewart Bridge continues to be rated at a 20-ton load limit and Lane County has no plans to replace this bridge.

To get there: Travel 1 mile east of Cottage Grove on Row River Road. Follow the sign to Mosby Creek Road by turning right, crossing the railroad tracks, then turning left to travel south. The bridge is located at the intersection of Mosby Creek and Garoutte Roads, 3½ miles from Cottage Grove.

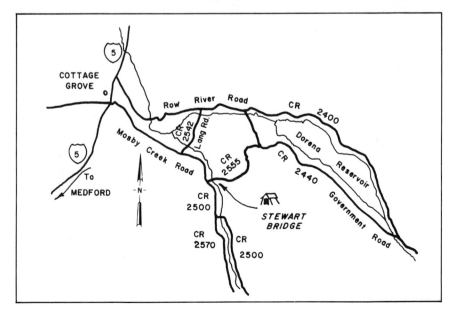

BRUMBAUGH BRIDGE

Stream: Mosby Creek
Built: 1948
World Guide No.: 37-20-29
T21S R2W S18
Truss: Howe
Length: 90 feet

The Brumbaugh Bridge was one of the last covered spans to be built in Lane County. It replaced a 92-foot Howe truss bridge built by Nels Roney in 1908. Although the current bridge was constructed in 1948 for $13,931, it was not housed until two years later when, instead of the usual wooden batten siding, metal siding was added. Only two other Oregon covered bridges are housed in metal.

Wooden pilings support the bridge instead of the usual concrete piers. Mosby Creek Bridge, only a few miles away, uses this same means of support. Horizontal wooden boards attached to the piers act to keep debris from accumulating around the piers during heavy stream flow.

The unusually wide portals on the Brumbaugh was an answer to criticism against small bridge openings. The bridge uses the standard 90-foot truss and state designed portals.

The Brumbaugh Bridge was named for early settlers in the area. At one time the stream which flows under the bridge was called Brumbaugh Creek, but the name was later changed to Mosby Creek.

To get there: Travel south of Cottage Grove on Mosby Creek Road for 6 miles at which point the road crosses Mosby Creek.

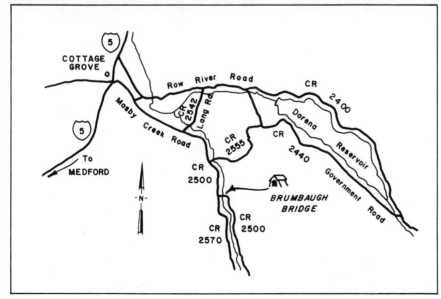

ERNEST BRIDGE

Stream: Mohawk River
Built: 1938
World Guide No.: 37-20-35
T16S R1W S5
Truss: Howe
Length: 75 feet

The Ernest Bridge may be in the best condition of any covered bridge in Lane County, but strangely not because of work done by the county bridge department. In the mid-1960s a movie company was filming *Shenandoah* in the Mohawk Valley area and needed a covered bridge for a particular scene. The movie company requested permission from the county to "alter" the bridge to reflect Civil War architecture, and promised to restore the bridge to equal or better condition, a promise which was kept. The bridge received new siding and paint in 1965.

The original covered bridge at this site was erected by A. N. Striker in 1903. That 83-foot span was named the Adams Bridge. When it was replaced in 1938 by Lane County, the $2,449.58 cost for construction included $72.00 for wrecking the old bridge.

The new bridge, with upper chord dimensions of 12″ x 12″ x 50 feet and lower dimensions of 12″ x 14″ x 81½ feet, was named after longtime residents of the area.

To get there: From Springfield, travel northeast to Marcola on Marcola Road. Three miles past Marcola turn right on Pachelke Road and travel ⅛ mile to the bridge.

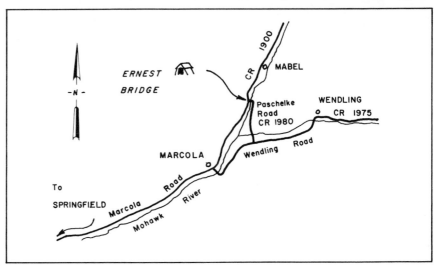

WENDLING BRIDGE
Stream: Mill Creek
Built: 1938
World Guide No.: 37-20-36
T16S R1W S10
Truss: Howe
Length: 60 feet

The Wendling Bridge appears to be hidden on a winding road northeast of Marcola.

In the 1890s, George X. Wendling, director of Booth-Kelly Lumber Company, established a post office in the small town which bears his name.

Cross planking on the bridge approaches rumble slightly as traffic passes over them. Like nearby Ernest Bridge, the Wendling Bridge shows faded, peeling circus posters pasted on its walls between the truss members.

Lane County spent only $2,241 to build the bridge in 1938. Like many other short span bridges in the county, it uses single piece chords for the Howe truss. The lower chords measure 12″ x 14″ x 65½ feet; the upper chords are 12″ x 12″ x 34 feet.

To get there: Follow 14th Street in Springfield northeast of Interstate 105, where it becomes Marcola Road, and travel to Marcola. Once in Marcola, turn east onto Wendling Road and follow it to the Wendling Bridge, only a short distance south of Wendling.

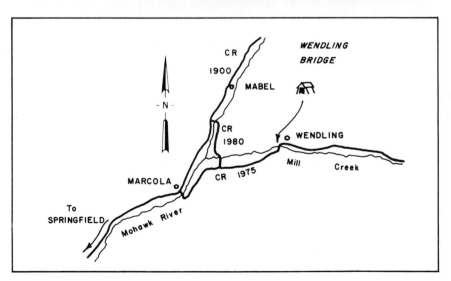

DEADWOOD BRIDGE

Stream: Deadwood Creek
Built: 1932
World Guide No.: 37-20-38
T16S R9W S25
Truss: Howe
Length: 105 feet

Deadwood Bridge is one of Oregon's most interesting covered bridges primarily because of the general disrepair of the structure.

Built in 1932 by Lane County at a cost of $4,814, the span was once considered to be a part of the State's secondary road system. One piece lower chord members, meauring 16″ x 16″ x 113 feet, give strength to the Howe truss construction.

Deadwood Creek allegedly received its name due to the abundance of large timber snags found in the area, the result of forest fires in the Coast Range. The primeval setting surrounding the bridge is suggestive of another place and time.

Both bridge portals have been splintered by high loads of log trucks and the bridge is in poor condition. Since heavy traffic has been rerouted onto a new concrete bridge nearby, the useful life of the bridge should be extended.

To get there: Travel north from Mapleton on Oregon Highway 36 (or southwest from Junction City) to the town of Deadwood. Follow the Deadwood Creek Road, located near the Lane County Highway shop. In 5 miles Deadwood Loop, on which the bridge is situated, connects from the east.

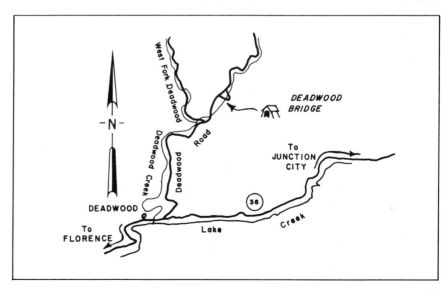

CHAMBERS BRIDGE
Stream: Coast Fork Willamette River
Built: 1936 (Private)
World Guide No.: 37-20-40
T20S R3W S32
Truss: Howe
Length: 78 feet

Chambers Bridge is the last covered railroad bridge in Oregon. It was built by the Oregon, Pacific and Eastern Railroad for a logging spur which brought logs to the Frank Chambers Mill in Cottage Grove. The sawmill burned in 1943. Although the bridge trusses are now exposed, at one time the sides were completely enclosed to afford maximum protection for the timbers.

In the typical construction for railroad spans, multiple steel reinforcing rods were used to hold truss members of herculean proportions necessary to support the moving weight of rail payloads. As in most wooden railroad bridges, three steel rods connect the upper and lower chords. The end vertical truss members, however, use five rods to hold them in place. Hand-hewn truss members in the Chambers Bridge, like others, were preferred over mill-sawed timbers because wood fibers crushed by saw teeth allowed moisture to enter more readily than axe formed surfaces.

The western approach to the bridge has been removed to make way for the easement of South River Road. Abandoned for years, the bridge has been a frequent target of arsonists as charred timbers attest. Fortunately, the bridge has not succumbed to fire.

Built to accommodate steam engines pulling logging trains, the sides of the Chambers Bridge stretch much higher than highway covered spans, almost hiding a rusting metal roof.

To get there: Travel to Cottage Grove and follow U.S. 99 (9th Street) to Main Street. Turn west and follow Main Street across the Coast Fork of the Willamette River. Before reaching the hospital, turn south onto South River Road. The Chambers Bridge is located ¼ mile south of this point.

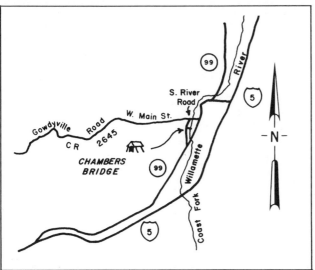

OFFICE BRIDGE

**Stream: North Fork of the Middle
         Fork, Willamette River**
Built: 1944
       Westfir Lumber Company
World Guide No.: 37-20-39
T21S R3E S7
Truss: Howe
Length: 180 feet

The Office Bridge spans a mill pond created by a dam on the North Fork of the Middle Fork of the Willamette River at the town of Westfir. The wooden span connected a lumber mill and its office—hence its name.

At 180 feet, it is Oregon's longest covered bridge. The present structure is a replacement of the original bridge at this location which washed out in 1942. The Westfir Lumber Company, which built the bridge, was purchased by Edward Hines Lumber Company of Chicago in 1945. In 1977, the company owned town of Westfir, the mill and the bridge were sold to an investment company.

A distinctive feature of the span is the covered walkway, separate from the roadway.

Built for carrying loaded log trucks, the truss members are of herculean proportions. The bridge is in the basic design of covered bridges built for railroad use, with multiple steel tension rods and compound chord members. Cross bracing on both the bottom and top chords adds rigidity to the structure.

To get there: Travel southeast of Eugene toward Oakridge on Oregon 58. From the west, turn onto Westridge Avenue, near milepost 31, continuing to Westfir. From the east, follow Harbor Drive, near milepost 33, to Westfir.

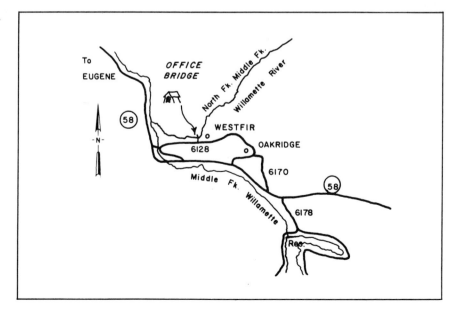

LINCOLN County

Settlers began to arrive in the coastal county in the 1860s. Elk City was settled by employees of the Corvallis and Yaquina Bay Road Compay in 1866, and the area became the first town in the county. Originally named Newton, the town was renamed Elk City in 1888 to honor the herds of elk roaming the area.

The community of Chitwood developed in the 1880s, named for Joshua Chitwood, the town's first postmaster. A school was built in 1887, but the town's activity reached its peak during the first World War. Two covered spans were built in the Chitwood area soon after the beginning of the Roaring Twenties. The Chitwood covered bridge still stands today. The nearby Thornton Creek Bridge was built in 1924, an 84-foot span just one mile west of the Chitwood roofed bridge, and uncertainty exists in assessing the costs and year built between the two bridges. The Thornton Creek Bridge is now gone.

Further south, the town of Fisher was settled in the 1890s, and the post office established in 1892. The town is named for a small fur bearing animal known locally as the fisher; the proper name being the marten. Two of the early postmasters were named Martin Johnson and S. W. Mink.

All over western Oregon roads were difficult to maintain in an usable condition, especially in the wet months. Wagon roads were a sea of mud in the winter, and dust a foot deep in the summer. Materials for road repair and bridge construction had to be obtained from nearby sources. Wood for bridges was often sawed at the bridge site or close by. Douglas fir was abundant and because the trees were so large, it was not difficult to get timber strong enough and sufficient in length to meet the requirements demanded by the construction of bridge trusses. Costs of the bridges were minimized by a standard style of design and construction. The moisture-filled atmosphere of coastal areas enhanced the need for protection of the bridge trusses. Lincoln County adopted a standard pattern of construction for its covered bridges, consisting of shingled roofs, rounded portals, flared sides, board-batten siding, the Howe truss, cross-wise plank flooring, and sometimes a coat of red paint.

An early covered bridge designer of the county was Andrew Porter, who designed such covered spans as the Schooner Creek Bridge three miles east of Taft, built in 1914. This structure lasted until the mid-1960s.

Perhaps the county's best known bridge builder was Otis Hamer, who worked on his first covered bridge in 1908. Between 1923 and 1937, he supervised crews which contructed sixteen roofed crossings. Hamer's crews varied from six to eight men who often camped at the bridge site for two or three months during the summer building seasons. The crews included three or four of his regular employees and the rest consisted of "locals" who needed work. Hamer and his crews worked on the Elk City Bridge in 1928, the metal Kernville Bridge in the late 1920s, the Yachats bridges during the early 1930s, and the Buck Creek Bridge in 1935. In 1930, he built the Rose Lodge covered bridge which spanned Slick Rock Creek until it was removed in the mid 1960s. Hamer's success as a bridge builder can be measured in part by the number of his bridges still standing. Lincoln County roofed bridges built by Hamer include the bridge at Chitwood, the Sams Creek Bridge near Siletz, the Five Rivers structure at Fisher, and the last covered bridge he built, the North Fork of the Yachats Bridge east of the town of Yachats. In addition, Polk County's covered bridge spanning Ritner Creek is a Hamer structure.

County funds are providing an added life to the bridges in use, as well as those bridges idly spanning streams next to modern concrete structures. As late as 1960, more than a dozen covered bridges in Lincoln County had daily use. Today, there are but six. Interest to keep the remaining roofed structures in good repair is adamant, according to county officials. At Fisher, the county recently invested about $2,000 to replace the rotting siding, hopefully adding years of life to the unused bridge. Residents of the area struggled in 1974 to keep the bridge standing for public enjoyment. Among the fighting supporters was Roy Olson, a relative of the brothers who provided the lumber that was used to enclose the trusses. The Olson family not only sawed the wood for the Fisher Bridge, but also cut the timbers for the Cascade Creek and the Birch Creek Bridges.

The Lincoln County bridges offer more interest to the photographer and artist as these covered bridges appear to show extra charm that many bridges in other counties don't exhibit.

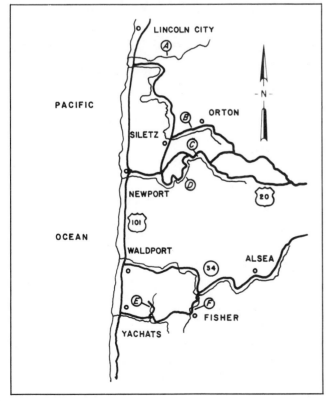

The Deer Creek Bridge. *Construction of the Deer Creek Bridge was completed in 1921. The 36-foot structure spanned the stream intersecting Lincoln County Road 568 near Salada until replaced by county crews in the 1950s. Nearly all the typical features of Lincoln County covered spans were exhibited in the Deer Creek structure. A shingle roof, flared batten-board siding, wooden pilings, and a curved portal design exist in most current Lincoln County covered spans.*

Photo: Oregon Highway Commission

A. *DRIFT CREEK*
B. *SAM'S CREEK*
C. *CHITWOOD*
D. *ELK CITY*
E. *YACHATS*
F. *FISHER*

SAM'S CREEK BRIDGE

Stream: Siletz River
Built: 1922
World Guide No.: 37-21-02
T10S R9W S6
Truss: Howe
Length: 100 feet

The Sam's Creek covered bridge, one of the Lincoln County spans now closed to vehicular traffic, was saved when the county built a new concrete bridge just a few feet away. The old wooden bridge is missing its east approach, and that end of the bridge is sealed with wire fencing, while the other approach restricts all but foot traffic.

Otis Hamer was awarded the contract to build the Sam's Creek Bridge in 1922, and when it was completed later that year, the bridge had cost just $4,000. Hamer recalled that the bridge was first called Spencer Scott Bridge to honor an Indian boy by that name living in the area. The boy was a daily visitor to view the progress and insisted upon being the first person to cross through the finished structure. Oddly, the bridge was built before the road leading to it was completed.

A nearby park, appropriately named Twin Bridge Memorial Park contains a loading ramp for boating, used frequently during fishing season.

To get there: From Newport, travel east on Highway 20 to Toledo; at Toledo, travel north on Highway 229 to Siletz. From Siletz, continue east toward Logsden approximately 5 miles. The bridge is on the right.

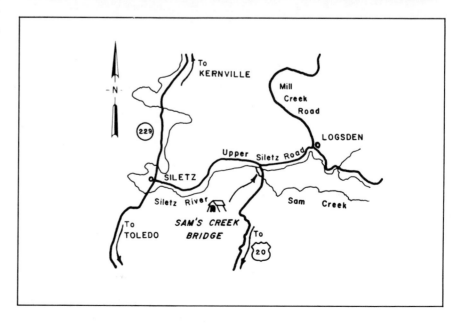

CHITWOOD BRIDGE

Stream: Yaquina River
Built: 1930
World Guide No.: 37-21-03
T10S R9W S32
Truss: Howe
Length: 96 feet

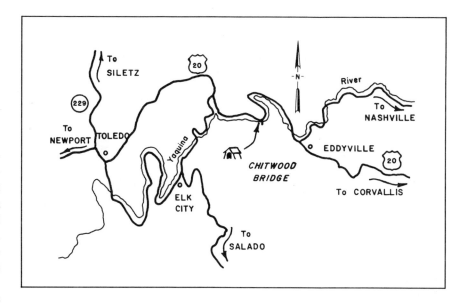

The bridge at Chitwood was once surrounded by stores, a post office, a telephone office, and several houses, but only the shell of the George Smith store next to the bridge remains, and that has been boarded up for years. Remnants of the Pepin Store, a competitor to Smith, stand on the opposite end of the covered bridge.

An excellent vein of sandstone was discovered near Chitwood in the early 1900s, and the Corvallis and Eastern Railroad ran a spur line from Chitwood into the quarry, causing an influx of workers for a few years. During this period, Chitwood became an important railstop for the smoking wood-burning trains from Yaquina to Corvallis, as the town was where the engines took on water and fuel, as well as passengers and freight.

Logging in the area once boomed enough to support not only the stores, but contributed to the rowdy times in the Chitwood Dance Hall as well. High speed transportation has dried up the businesses, causing Chitwood to remain only as a ghost town.

To get there: From Newport, take Highway 20 east past Toledo, and continue on Highway 20 for 2½ miles past the Elk City Road. Chitwood Bridge is on the right, near mile post 17.

ELK CITY BRIDGE

Stream: Yaquina River
Built: 1922
World Guide No.: 37-21-05
T11S R10W S14
Truss: Howe
Length: 100 feet

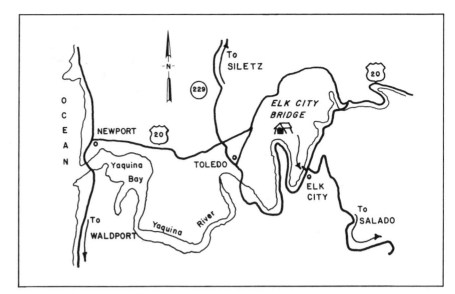

When built in 1922, the Elk City covered bridge cost the county but $3,200. The bridge carried passengers to the train depot on the other side of the Yaquina River, but now dead-ends to through traffic. Once painted red, the bridge paint has all but faded, leaving a rustic-looking structure.

Elk City, at one time a booming partner of Chitwood, had a saloon, a hotel, a store, a fraternal lodge, and rental cabins, giving it an appearance of a real town. The old grocery is the only business operating, and the store adds to the atmosphere of the river community. Floods carried away the saw mill and the hotel, and neither has been rebuilt. The apparent remaining resource is the fishing, which helps to keep the cabins rented during fishing season. The bridge is nine miles by river from Toledo and just three miles by air. The tidewater ends just three miles above the bridge.

To get there: From Newport, travel east on Highway 20 to Toledo, and continue into town. Turn right onto Main Street, then right again onto First Street. Turn left onto Butler Bridge Road, and continue on this road to Elk City. Or from Chitwood, travel west 2½ miles to Elk City Road, then travel about 5 miles to Elk City.

NORTH FORK OF THE YACHATS BRIDGE

Stream: N. Fork of the Yachats River
Built: 1938
World Guide No.: 37-21-08
T14S R11W S26
Truss: Queenpost
Length: 42 feet

The rustic covered bridge spanning the North Fork of the Yachats cost the county just $1,500 when built in 1938, and today, it is one of shortest covered spans in the state. This wooden bridge was the last covered span constructed by veteran bridge builder, Otis Hamer.

Located just seven miles from the salt water of the Pacific Ocean, this trim little bridge is one of the few to escape the "graffiti-artists" so common in many of the other covered bridges. Warnings nailed on the ends of the bridge tell of a long-forgotten regulation, "No Cleated Tractors."

Although this queenpost-design of bridge appears in excellent condition, the county has put a load limit for its passengers at 8 tons. Most of the siding has been replaced in recent years, and the structure appears able to enjoy many more years of service. As with other Lincoln County spans, hand-split pilings support the bridge.

The nearby community was established in 1880 as Ocean View, and was later changed to Yachats in 1916 in honor of a local tribe of Indians. The name "Yachats," according to the Indians means, "At the foot of the mountain," an appropriate nomenclature for both the bridge and community.

To get there: From Yachats, go east on Yachats River Road approximately seven miles. After crossing a cement bridge, turn left, and travel about 2 miles on this road to the bridge.

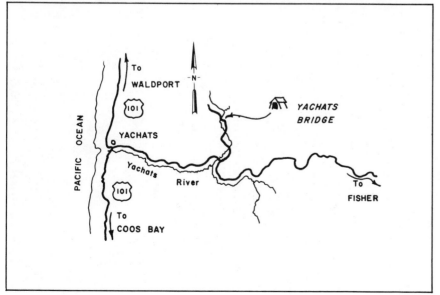

FISHER SCHOOL BRIDGE (Five Rivers)

Stream: Five Rivers
Built: 1919
World Guide No.: 37-21-11
T15S R10W S1
Truss: Howe
Length: 72 feet

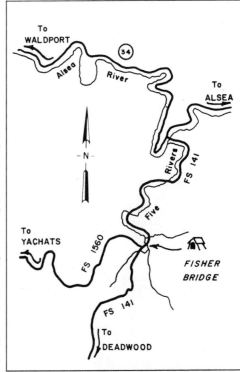

The Fisher Bridge is located in the rugged foothills of Lincoln County where isolation from the rushing traffic is a welcome relief. Recent remodeling included replacement of the rotting siding, costing the county as much as the original construction. The bridge is now closed to vehicles, and a modern, concrete bridge nearby handles daily traffic.

Otis Hamer contracted to build the wooden structure for approximately $2,500. According to George A. Melvin, a workman on the bridge, a group of farmers aided in construction of the covered span in 1919. The builders cut the larger trees in the vicinity, and then shaped them into logs by hand with the use of broadaxes. After the main framework was completed, it was enclosed with lumber cut at the small saw mill operated by the Olsen brothers—Oscar, William, and Roy. Originally, the bridge was painted red, but prior to the replacement of the exterior siding, only traces of the red paint remained.

The structure spans Five Rivers, so named because of the five streams of Alder Creek, Cougar Creek, Buck Creek, Crab Creek, and Cherry Creek which make up the stream. The area surrounding Fisher was the site of other covered bridges. The Buck Creek Bridge, a 36-foot span was constructed in 1924 just 2½ miles north of Fisher; and the Cascade Creek structure, also a 36-foot design was built in 1927 just 2 miles west of Fisher. Only the Five Rivers bridge remains.

To get there: It is recommended that you take Highway 34 east from Waldport for approximately 20 miles to the Fisher-Five Rivers Road. At the fork at Siletz Road, continue left past Buck Creek Road for about one mile. The bridge is on the right. An alternate route is one from Yachats east over 20 miles of extremely rough road, and this route is not recommended without a map and a well-conditioned vehicle.

UPPER DRIFT CREEK BRIDGE

Stream: Upper Drift Creek
Built: 1914
World Guide No.: 37-21-14
T7S R11W S36
Truss: Howe
Length: 66 feet

Said by the Oregon Highway Department to be the oldest covered bridge in the Oregon list of covered bridges, the Upper Drift Creek Bridge remains boarded from traffic, with a modern span just a few yards downstream. Located approximately 1½ miles from the coast line, this bridge is closer to the Pacific Ocean than any other roofed wooden bridge. When built, the covered structure cost about $1,800.

A recently installed sign states: "Foot traffic only" and the wooden planking allows pedestrians through the bridge to hear the hollow-echoing footsteps so common in the Lincoln County covered bridges. The old bridge retains the usual cedar shingle roof, wooden flooring, and the flared batten-board siding constructed of Douglas fir. In 1965, the Lincoln County passed an edict preserving the covered bridge indefinitely as a historical memorial to the Lincoln County pioneers.

When the bridge was built in 1914, the community surrounding the bridge site was known as Lutgens and in 1917, the name was changed to Nice. In all, at least eight name changes occurred in this community prior to the closing of the post office in 1919.

To get there: From Lincoln City, travel south on Highway 101 three miles to Drift Creek Road, and then travel east for 1½ miles. Turn right and continue for ½ mile to the bridge.

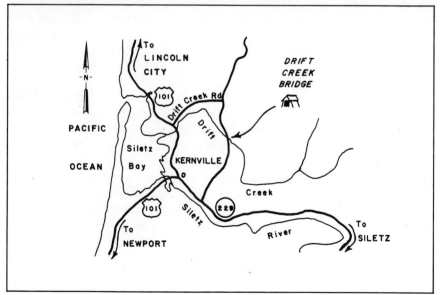

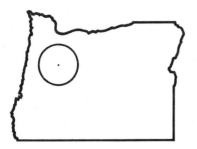

LINN County

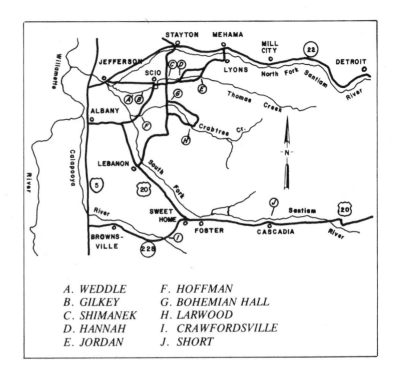

A. WEDDLE   F. HOFFMAN
B. GILKEY   G. BOHEMIAN HALL
C. SHIMANEK   H. LARWOOD
D. HANNAH   I. CRAWFORDSVILLE
E. JORDAN   J. SHORT

In 1845, John Crabtree received the area's first Donation Land Claim for property near the present town of Crabtree. Soon afterward, he and his wife became the parents of the first twins born in the Oregon Territory. The nearby area expanded with pioneers pouring in from the east and midwest. The Providence Church near Crabtree was established in 1853, and Joab Powell, the powerful and dynamic circuit-riding preacher, was the first pastor of the church. Powell, who was unable to read or write, persuaded his wife to read the Bible to him until he memorized the passages for his sermons. Powell chewed tobacco and wore baggy clothes even on Sundays. The "hell-fire" preacher would start his sermon in a home spun manner, "I take my text from the one-eyed chapter of the two-eyed John." He then began to preach in such a swaying manner that those who came to scoff remained to pray. When invited to give the invocation at an early legislative session, Joab Powell was said to have uttered one of the shortest official prayers spoken before a governmental gathering: "Forgive them Lord, for they know not what they do."

The town of Scio developed in 1866 on the banks of Thomas Creek, at the site of a grist mill. A covered bridge spanned the creek at Scio until the bridge's replacement in 1912. Prior to its destruction, the covered bridge aided three members of the city's Women's Temperance League to dispose of liquor when the women raided the nearby saloon and rolled several barrels of whiskey off the bridge into Thomas Creek.

Ten covered bridges grace the Linn County streams today, and all but one is open to vehicular traffic. Five of these bridges are over Thomas Creek, the most spans crossing over a single stream in Oregon. In the 1960s, fourteen covered bridges could be counted in the county. Two of these, the Hufford and Foster roofed structures were removed during construction of dams in the area.

The bridge design for Linn County roofed structures prior to 1930 featured squared portals having angled ends. About 1930, Linn County adopted the Oregon Highway Department plan for rounded portals and partially exposed truss designs. The state design enables the wooden bridge to appear more than just a box above the water. The open truss style allows more light and visibility to the traveller, and allows wind resistance to be kept to a minimum. Even with the partially exposed trusses, the wetness does little damage. According to Linn County engineers, the partially exposed trusses enables faster drying of the wood than the enclosed designs adopted by other counties. It has been discovered that most of the wetness is from the spray of water from passing traffic. This moisture has been minimized by enclosing the inside lower portion of the trusses with a wooden partition to repel the spray.

Maintenance expenses of the Linn County bridges plague the county officials, and the alternatives to offset the costs are limited. Public sentiment is high concerning saving the bridges from replacement; however, the sentiment is lessened regarding the prospects of funding repair and upkeep costs.

Sadly, the prospects of keeping the nine operating bridges open to traffic are dim. The Weddle Bridge is scheduled for closure shortly, and probably will remain open to pedestrian traffic only. The Gilkey covered bridge appears to be next, and further upstream on Thomas Creek, either the Jordan Bridge or the Hannah Bridge will be replaced with a concrete structure to facilitate the increased logging traffic in that area. Two other covered structures, Bohemian Hall and Shimanek, are located on a Federal Aid Secondary road which is scheduled for widening in the 1980s, so the removal of these two bridges may be accomplished at that time. Rerouting of traffic will ensure a longer life for the Larwood, Short, and Hoffman covered bridges.

The Bates Park Bridge. *An oddity in Oregon covered bridge construction was featured at the Bates Park Bridge spanning the South Santiam River near Sweet Home. The river crossing actually consisted of two separate bridges, 154 feet total in length. The near span was built in 1923 and painted red. The other bridge was built seven years later and was painted white. Construction of the older red span followed the old Linn County style of portal openings angled at the tops, and portal boarding being horizontal instead of vertical. The newer span was designed by the State Highway Commission and exhibited a different portal design, windows, and a concrete foundation. Until 1958, when the red bridge was replaced, Bates Park remained a double-span structure. A modern concrete span needing only a minimal amount of maintenance replaced the other roofed wooden bridge in 1970.*

Photo: Salem Public Library, Ben Maxwell Collection

JORDAN BRIDGE
Stream: Thomas Creek
Built: 1937
World Guide No.: 37-22-01
T10S R1E S4
Truss: Howe
Length: 90 feet

The covered bridge at Jordan is the most northern of the Linn County roofed spans. It is located not far from the site of the old post office established in the area in 1874. Although the county road is moderately travelled, the bridge appears to be in good condition, except for a missing skirting board or two. The bridge typifies the practice of partially exposing trusses, a feature unique to Linn County. In recent years, the portal has been enlarged to facilitate larger loads and faster traffic.

Thomas Creek, which is spanned by the covered bridge, was the site for a dam, a cheese factory, two mills, a power plant for Scio, and a general store. Unusual rock formations can still be seen below the dam. The bridge leads from Highway 226 to a community in the hills bearing the name of Jordan. Joab Powell, a pioneer circuit rider, named Jordan Valley to commemorate a valley in the holy land. Years ago, a monastery was maintained up in the hills above the community.

To get there: From Salem, travel east on Highway 22 to Lyons, then continue approximately six miles southwest along Thomas Creek to the bridge.

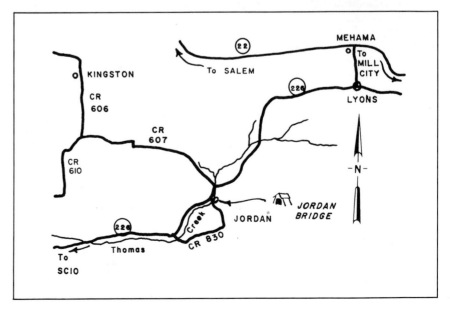

HANNAH BRIDGE

Stream: Thomas Creek
Built: 1936
World Guide No.: 37-22-02
T10S R1E S8
Truss: Howe
Length: 105 feet

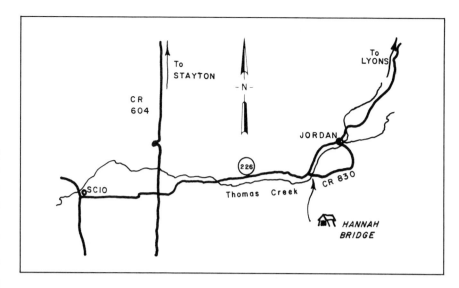

Hannah Bridge is another example of leaving trusses partially exposed by open sides. Although there is no apparent cost savings, the improved vision for drivers, and a more pleasing appearance are the advantages of this type of design.

Several years ago, the Thomas Y store and gasoline station existed close by, but have since closed. (The price on the now empty gas pump was noted to be 34.9 cents per gallon!)

The Hannah Bridge spans Thomas Creek just 1½ miles downstream from the Jordan covered bridge. Thomas Creek is named for Frederick Thomas, who obtained a Donation Land Claim and settled on the banks of the stream in 1846.

To get there: From Scio, travel 6½ miles east to County Road 830. Turn right onto Road 830. The bridge is only 100 feet from Highway 226. Or from Mehama (Highway 22), travel south to Lyons and take Highway 226 approximatley 8 miles to the bridge. (You will pass Jordan Bridge on the way.)

SHIMANEK BRIDGE

Stream: Thomas Creek
Built: 1966
World Guide No.: 37-22-03
T10S R1W S10
Truss: Howe
Length: 130 feet

Another of the Thomas Creek bridges, Shimanek offers an exception to the usual open sided structure and rounded portal. Several features are exhibited at this bridge. Red paint, the old style portal design, and louvered windows are found on no other bridge in Linn County. Rods in the truss design are grouped into a series of four rods instead of the usual three rods at each stress point.

The first bridge built in this location is believed to have been constructed as early as 1861, while the first documented covered bridge was built in 1891 for a cost of $1,150. In 1904, the county rebuilt the bridge, but it later washed out in 1921. Its replacement lasted until 1927, when high water damaged the piers and the span was replaced. Trees were blown against the fourth covered bridge at this site during the Columbus Day Storm of 1962. Wind damage forced the county to restrict the old wooden bridge to a 2-ton load limit with single lane traffic. The bridge was destroyed soon after, and in 1966, the current Shimanek Bridge was completed, the fifth covered bridge to occupy this site.

It has been rumored that the 1891 bridge had a welcome accommodation of a two-hole toilet built into the foundation. The current bridge does not feature the luxury of a toilet, but does have the honor of being the county's youngest covered bridge.

The name Shimanek comes from the family of community leaders who lived near the bridge since the early 1900s.

To get there: From Scio, take Highway 226 east 2 miles to Richardson Gap Road (County Road 637). Turn left, and continue ¾ mile to the bridge.

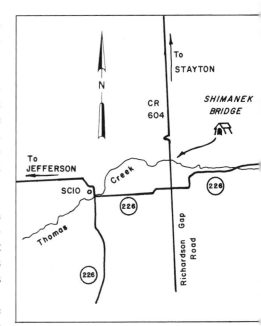

GILKEY BRIDGE

Stream: Thomas Creek
Built: 1939
World Guide No.: 37-22-04
T10S R2W S23
Truss: Howe
Length: 120 feet

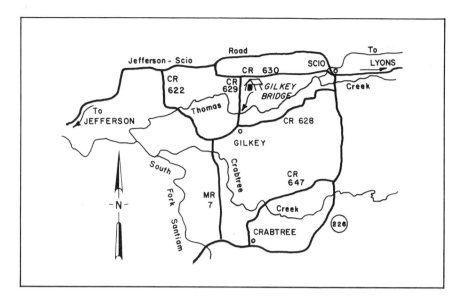

This covered span is another of the Thomas Creek bridges, and until 1960, it proudly stood next to a covered railroad bridge.

Gilkey was once a town of some activity, and a nearby sign states: "Gilkey Station was established when the railroad arrived in 1880 and was named in honor of Allen and William Gilkey. Gilkey served as a shipping point for farm products." Just about all but the sign and bridge are now gone.

Sadly, this roofed structure has lost several skirting boards and the roof has several metal sheets missing. The familiar swimming rope is tied to the framework of the bridge, and during the summer swimmers enjoy this area of Thomas Creek, too.

Increased traffic may force the county to realign or replace the bridge in the near future.

To get there: From Scio, take Highway 226 south for one-half mile and turn right onto County Road 628. Travel approximately 3 miles west on Road 628 to the intersection of County Road 629. Turn right onto Road 629 and travel ½ mile to the bridge. Or from Scio, take County Road 630 west for 3 miles to the intersection of Road 629. Turn left onto Road 629 and travel south for 1¼ miles to the bridge.

WEDDLE BRIDGE
(Devaney Bridge)

Stream: Thomas Creek
Built: 1937
World Guide No.: 37-22-05
T10S R2W S21
Truss: Howe
Length: 120 feet

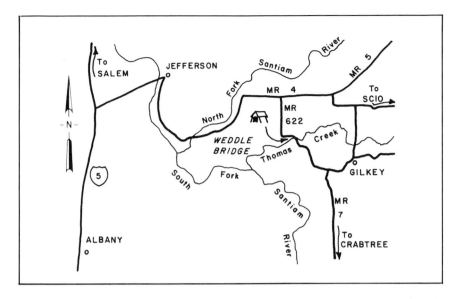

Linn County officials indicate that the Weddle covered bridge spanning Thomas Creek two miles east of Gilkey will be the next covered structure to be by-passed. A new concrete span ¼ mile downstream will handle vehicular traffic, but the old wooden bridge will allow foot traffic to enjoy the walk through its portals.

Although built in 1937, increased logging and farming traffic has reduced the expected life, as the expense of repairs is now too great to be practical.

Linn County and local residents disagree on the name of the bridge. Residents in the area prefer "Devaney," but the county renamed the bridge "Weddle" for the nearby Weddle Ranch.

To get there: From Albany, travel north on Interstate 5 to the Jefferson exit. Travel east to Jefferson on U.S. 99E. At Jefferson, turn right onto South Main Street (Scio road) and travel approximately 3½ miles to County Road 622. Turn right onto Road 622 and travel for 1½ mile to the bridge. Or from Scio, take Market Road 4 west (through West Scio) approximately 5 miles to Road 622. Turn left onto Road 622.

LARWOOD BRIDGE
Stream: Crabtree Creek
Built: 1939
World Guide No.: 37-22-06
T11S R1E S7
Truss: Howe
Length: 105 feet

Larwood Bridge was built to Highway Commission specifications. The 105 foot length, partially exposed trusses, white-washed interior, and rounded portal shape were features outlined by the state plans. The asphalt covering laid over the cross wise deck planking cuts down the vibration and should add years of use to the structure.

This covered span is located three miles north of Lacomb, spanning Crabtree Creek next to Larwood Wayside Park. Roaring River, which empties into Crabtree Creek near the bridge, is the only river to flow into a creek, an oddity in U.S. geography that was featured in Ripley's BELIEVE IT OR NOT. The Larwood community was named for William T. Larwood, the first postmaster of the post office established in 1893.

Local residents most often refer to the bridge as the Roaring River Covered Bridge.

To get there: From Scio, take Oregon 226 east to Richardson Gap Road; follow Richardson Gap Road south for 3 miles to County Road 643. Take Road 643 east approximately 4 miles to the bridge.

BOHEMIAN HALL BRIDGE
(Richardson Gap)

Stream: Crabtree Creek
Built: 1947
World Guide No.: 37-22-07
T10S R1W S34
Truss: Howe
Length: 120 feet

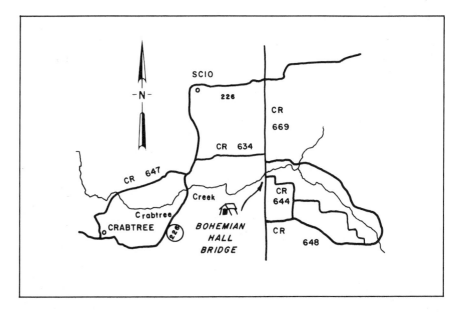

The Bohemian Hall roofed bridge, located five miles southeast of Scio on Crabtree Creek, is one the three Oregon covered bridges housed entirely in sheet metal. This metal and wood cross-breed takes its name from the nearby Tolstoj ZCBJ Lodge, located just north of the bridge. In 1922, emigrants from Czechoslovakia founded the community surrounding the bridge site. The lodge was built, giving the area residents a place for dances and meetings until vandalism caused the hall to be closed.

Holes in the bridge from rifle bullets indicate that the structure is an easy target for destructive individuals. Additionally, some of the roof's metal sheets are missing, apparently from strong winds. Linn County recently replaced the approaches and the railings, adding new life of the bridge and safety for the traffic. The cost of these repairs exceeded $10,000. This span is one of the two Linn County covered bridges built by a private contractor and not by the county.

Local residents prefer the long-time name of "Richardson Gap Bridge" over that of the more recent county name of "Bohemian Hall." The Richardson family settled in the area between Thomas Creek and Crabtree Creek prior to 1880.

To get there: From Scio, take Highway 226 east for approximately two miles to Richardson Gap Road. Take Richardson Gap Road south for 3½ miles to the bridge.

HOFFMAN BRIDGE

Stream: Crabtree Creek
Built: 1936
World Guide No.: 37-22-08
T11S R2W S2
Truss: Howe
Length: 90 feet

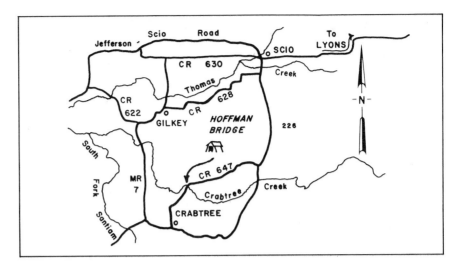

This covered bridge spans Crabtree Creek one mile northeast of the town of Crabtree on the flats below Hungry Hill. Both the town and creek were named in honor of John Crabtree who settled in the area in 1845.

Gothic-style windows grace this structure instead of the usual open Linn County truss design. A protective metal strip has been added to the upstream side of the bridge to keep debris and highwater from damaging the lower portion of the bridge siding. The portal design, originally rounded when the bridge was constructed, was enlarged and squared to allow passage of larger loads. The bridge today exhibits a metal roof, and the abutments consist of wooden pilings.

The roofed river crossing was built by Lee Hoffman following State Highway specifications in 1936. The structure is one of the few Linn County covered bridges scheduled to be kept in use indefinitely, and the span appears to be in excellent condition.

To get there: From Albany, take U.S. 20 to Crabtree. At Crabtree, take County Road 647 north for approximately 1 mile to the bridge. Or from Scio, travel south on Highway 226 for approximately 3 miles to County Road 647. Travel west for about 2 miles to the bridge.

SHORT BRIDGE

Stream: South Fork Santiam River
Built: 1945
World Guide No.: 37-22-09
T13S R2E S36
Truss: Howe
Length: 105 feet

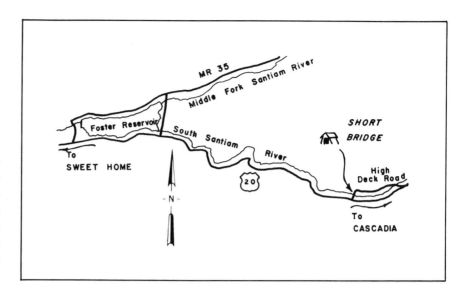

The Short Bridge is the sole survivor of the South Fork of the Santiam River covered bridges, and is one of the few remaining to have a wooden shingle roof. Although the peeling paint makes the bridge appear older than its age, the railings and approaches were recently renovated.

When the wooden-housed structure was built, the bridge was known more commonly as the Whiskey Butte Bridge, but was renamed for a long-time area resident, Gordon Short. The bridge is not scheduled for replacement and will serve the logging interests in the area.

The drive along the South Santiam River from Sweet Home to Cascadia truly makes the trip to Short Bridge enjoyable. Foster Reservoir, Green Peter Dam, and the ghost town of Quartzville surround the bridge site.

To get there: Take U.S. Highway 20 to Sweet Home and continue east past Foster Dam toward Cascadia. Near the city limits of Cascadia, turn off Highway 20 at High Deck Road. The bridge is just off the highway on High Deck Road.

CRAWFORDSVILLE BRIDGE

Stream: Calapooia River
Built: 1932
World Guide No.: 37-22-15
T14S R1W S18
Truss: Howe
Length: 105 feet

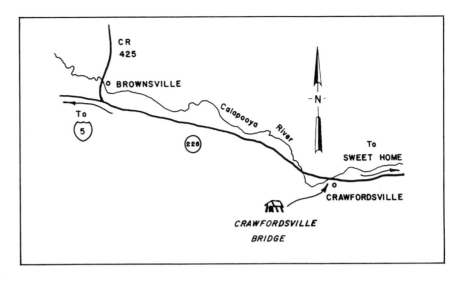

The bridge at Crawfordsville displays another version of Linn County's open truss style. The roofed span, built in 1932, shows a narrow slit window on both sides of the structure. The Crawfordsville span exhibited rounded portals until they were enlarged by State Highway employees to allow larger loads.

After completion of the bridge, Linn County turned the structure over to the state when the road was designated as a state highway. When the bridge was by-passed in 1963, the state relinquished control, and returned the bridge back to the road department of the county. Title was then passed to the Linn County Parks Department when the bridge was left standing, and today a park commemorates the historical significance of the old wooden structure.

The bridge at Crawfordsville spans Calapooia River eight miles southeast of Brownsville on Highway 228. The area was named in honor of Philemon V. Crawford who settled in the area, and on whose land the town was established in the 1870s.

To get there: From Brownsville, take Oregon 228 southeast 8 miles to Crawfordsville. The highway crosses Calapooia River just a few feet from the covered bridge.

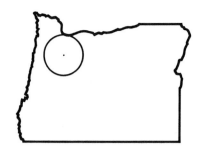

MARION County

Marion county covered bridges were more utilitarian in concept and purpose.

Earlier county bridges were left unpainted after they were constructed. Later bridges in the county received a coat of red barn paint. One of the last of the red bridges to be replaced was the Turner Bridge, less than a mile east of the town. Like most covered spans in the county, it cost the taxpayers less than $4,000. The Gallon House structure cost $1,310 when constructed in 1916-1917, and its sister bridge, the Coleman Bridge, spanning Abiqua Creek, cost just $1,310 when built in 1927. The Pudding River near Barlow was crossed by a 100-foot covered bridge, built in 1915. The bridge served the travellers for almost 40 years with relatively minor repairs. It was built practically on the line between Clackamas and Marion Counties, so that some of the maintenance had been carried out by each county. The last known covered span constructed in Marion County was the Slater Bridge over Abiqua Creek, built in the early 1930s and was replaced in 1954.

Advancing technology and increased traffic reduced the covered bridge numbers of Marion County to the lone survivor at Silverton. Prior to World War II, a dozen covered spans were standing at places like Turner, Scotts Mills, Stayton, Taylor's Grove on the Little North Fork of the Santiam River, and Silverton. Two of the North Fork of the Santiam River bridges spanning the water between Marion and Linn counties were replaced prior to 1940. The Mill City Bridge lasted until 1934, and the Gates Bridge, a 174-foot structure, was replaced in 1938.

Bridges were built in Marion County in the 1850s, but difficulty exists in determining if they were covered. Many bridges constructed in the 1850s were built on a co-operative basis. The community raised half the cost and the rest was supplied by the county. Ornate penmanship in the early commissioner's journals is beautiful, but hard to read, and although these journals mention the construction of several bridges, they do not indicate any to be covered prior to 1862. The journals do reveal, however, that Daniel Clark and John Hayden signed a contract on April 16, 1862 to build a covered span to cross Pringle Creek. The bridge construction was completed in September of that year following specifications prepared by A. R. Stoughten. That 200-foot span replaced an earlier uncovered bridge built in 1856 at the Salem location. During the 1880s, Salem newspapers complained about an accumulation of filth in the bridge that never seemed to get cleaned out. Public sentiment sided with the replacement of the covered span, which occurred following the flood of 1890.

Marion County covered bridges were rarely impressive in design. Most were nothing more than a shed with opening at either end, and were built over a wooden bridge. One historian said, "County courts, often impecunious and sometimes parsimonious, were indisposed toward spending county monies for the sake of distinction or embellishment."

The Scotts Mills Bridge. Thomas McKay, once an employee of the Hudson's Bay Company, established a grist mill and a saw mill on Butte Creek, the site of Scotts Mills in 1853. This 1941 picture shows the plainness of design of Marion County covered bridges. Enclosing the county spans was designed only for the sake of extended durability, and not for beauty. The roofed model at Scotts Mills was dismantled after being damaged by a logging truck in the late 1940s.

Photo: Salem Public Library, Ben Maxwell Collection

GALLON HOUSE BRIDGE

Stream: Abiqua Creek
Built: 1916-17
World Guide No.: 37-24-01
T6S R1W S22
Truss: Howe
Length: 84 feet

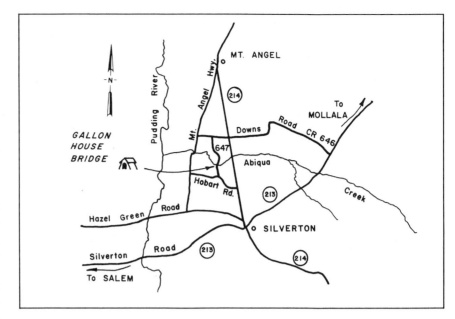

Gallon House Bridge, the last of the Marion county covered bridges, is located on County Road No. 647 about 1.4 miles northwest of Silverton, over Abiqua Creek. The name, Gallon House, was due to the fact that the bridge was used as a "pigeon drop." An old liquor dispensary opened up at the north entrance of the bridge and the operators used to sell "white lightning" whiskey there because during that time, Silverton was "dry" and Mt. Angel was "wet." The Gallon House was located in Mt. Angel territory.

The old roofed bridge is supported by wooden pilings. Wooden approaches, plank floorings, and a shingle roof are features of the covered structure. A narrow daylighting strip just below the roof line helps illuminate the bridge interior.

During the 1964-65 flood, the bridge suffered considerable damage. The County Board of Commissioners, however, decided that the bridge should be repaired and kept as a historical landmark, as it is the only covered bridge in Marion County.

To get there: From Salem, travel north on Highway 213 (Silverton Road) to Silverton. At Silverton, travel north on Highway 214 approximately ½ mile to Hobart Road. Turn west (left) on Hobart Road and continue for 1 mile to Gallon House Road. Turn north (right) onto Gallon House Road and travel ½ mile to the bridge. Or from Mt. Angel, travel south 1½ miles to Downs Road. Turn west onto Downs Road and continue ½ mile to Gallon House Road. Turn south (left) onto Gallon House Road and continue ½ mile to the bridge.

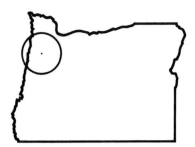

POLK County

Polk County was named for James K. Polk, and organized as a county December 22, 1845. Dallas, on the La Creole River (later renamed Rickreall Creek) was designated as the county seat in 1850-51, and incorporated in 1874. Other towns developing in the 1850s included Eola, Monmouth, Buena Vista, Bethel, and Luckiamute.

Public road construction began in the 1840s, with petitioners asking the courts for public roads as soon as the necessary twelve households were obtained. As roads developed, the demand for durable and safe bridges became a foremost concern. By the early 1900s, nearly every major bridge was a covered span.

Early county bridge builders included St. John and Stone, R. M. Gilbert, C. F. Royal and Son, and Ira Mehrling. The firm of St. John and Stone was awarded such contracts as the Soup Creek Bridge for $1,250 in 1884. In 1895, the contract to build the Hagood covered span in the city of Dallas was awarded to St. John and Stone. Just one year later, R. M. Gilbert built a covered bridge on Lee Rowell Road to span the Yamhill River for a cost of $394.23. The Hooker Bridge contract was awarded to C. F. Royal and Son on September 3, 1903 for a low bid of $900, provided that the county furnish the chords for the Luckiamute River Bridge.

Early commissioner's journals indicated the county advertised for bids concerning bridge repair as well as initial construction. Repair of the Hagood Bridge at Dallas was completed by J. F. Teal for $19.50 in 1899. Teal was the low bidder. During the same year, the re-roofing contract of the Wallace covered structure was given to C. F. Royal and Son for the low bid of $68.

Bids were sometimes modified by the county court. When the advertising of bids for the Bagley Bridge was presented in 1906, the notice called for three different plans and specifications. The court asked for bids representing spans of 75 feet, 91 feet, and 100 feet, with the right to reject any or all bids. The contract was awarded to Mehrling and Ferguson, who bid $1,068 to build a 75 foot span with allowances for approaches costing $2.20 per lineal foot.

One of the later covered bridge builders in the county was Otis Hamer, who recalled that his Ritner Creek Bridge required over 40,000 feet of lumber for its construction and cost more than $6,000. The actual cost was $6,960. The roofed bridge, built in 1927, replaced an unhoused structure at the same site.

An end of covered bridge construction took place officially in Polk County in the 1930s when the late Judge G. L. Hawkins stated that his county would no longer build covered bridges as they were unsafe. "They're a hazard to modern and speedy traffic," he said.

The technological advances occurring in the twentieth century decimated the covered bridge numbers to a duo of survivors, the Ritner Creek Bridge and the Dallas Pumping Station Bridge.

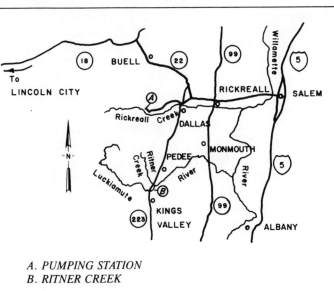

A. PUMPING STATION
B. RITNER CREEK

The Blair Bridge. *The Blair span, crossing Mill Creek near Buell, typified early Polk County features of bridge design. This structure was built in 1906 at a cost of just $714. It lasted until the late 1940s. Shingled roofs, narrow daylighting strips, board and batten siding, and wooden pilings were construction specifications required by the county court. Sometimes a coat of paint was included, but most often it was not. Many covered spans, therefore appeared older than their age due to early weathering.*

Photo: Salem Public Library, Ben Maxwell Collection

RITNER CREEK BRIDGE

Stream: Ritner Creek
Built: 1927
World Guide No.: 37-27-01
T10S R6W S5
Truss: Howe
Length: 75 feet

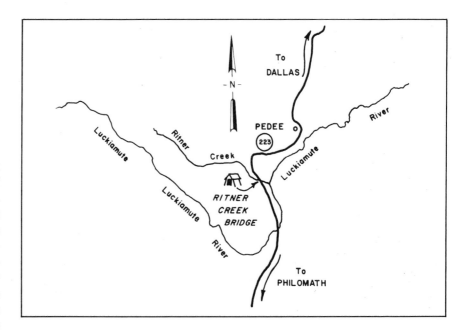

Until March, 1976, the Ritner Creek covered bridge was the sole survior of the Oregon State Highway covered structures. It was removed from that status when two huge cranes lifted the bridge from its abutments to a new location about 60 feet downstream. Involvement of students and other county residents helped save the bridge when the State Highway Division planned to replace it because it was too narrow and dangerous for the weight and speed of highway traffic.

Voters in Polk County approved a $29,000 one-time levy to save the bridge, and a $2,000 annual continuing levy to maintain the bridge and a wayside park in the surrounding area.

This well-preserved example of a Howe truss bridge is located just two miles south of Pedee on Ritner Creek, on State Highway 223. The bridge was constructed in 1926-27 by Hamer and Curry Contractors at a cost of $6,963.78. The portals, once rounded, were cut square in the early 1960s to accommodate taller trucks. Another feature includes the use of gothic-styled windows on either side of the bridge to daylight the bridge interior.

Residents in the area can remember the inside of the bridge as a convenient place to install their mail boxes.

To get there: From Dallas, travel south on Highway 223 through Pedee: continue for approximately 2 miles south on 223 to the bridge site.

DALLAS PUMPING STATION BRIDGE

Stream: Rickreall Creek
Built: 1915-16
World Guide No.: 37-27-02
T7S R6W S35
Truss: Howe
Length: 84 feet

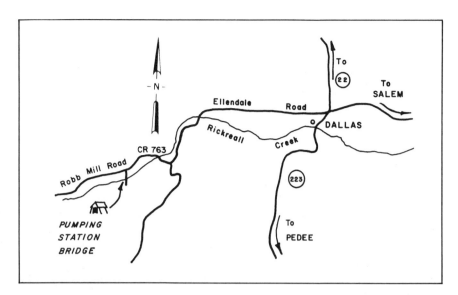

At least two distinctions "favor" the Dallas Pumping Station covered bridge. It is the narrowest of the Oregon Covered bridges, and the least beautiful. The rusting corrugated metal covering the roof and sides manages to protect the vital truss members, but pieces of the metal can be found downstream in Rickreall Creek. The bridge was used for traffic crossing the stream serving the Dallas Water Works. The extremely narrow width had limited the usage throughout past years. A locked metal gate prevents visitors from passing through the bridge.

The Pumping Station roofed bridge was built in 1915-16 by the Dallas Water Company, a private company owned and operated by H. V. Gates.

According to Ray Boydston, a retired employee of the company, the total cost of construction was less than $1,000.

To get there: From Dallas, travel west on Ellendale Road No. 20 for approximately 2½ miles to Robb Mill Road No. 763. On Robb Mill Road (private), continue for about 2 miles, following the creek to the bridge site. The bridge is on the left.

The History

WHY BRIDGES ARE COVERED

The question is eventually raised by almost everyone who sees a covered bridge: "Why are bridges covered?"

An old timer, with tongue-in-cheek, once replied, "Our bridges were covered for the same reason that our belles wore hoop skirts and crinolines—to protect the structural beauty that is seldom seen, but nevertheless appreciated."

The basic reason for covering truss-supported spans was to protect the truss and chord timbers: covered seasoned trusses lasted up to five times longer than open spans, because moisture that could cause the wood to rot was kept out of critical joints.

Other reasons for covering bridges have been given, some of questionable validity:

City fathers alleged they were covered to hide shoddy workmanship so that taxpayers couldn't see what a poor job contractors had done.

Farmers said that the portals of covered bridges served to round out the hay on a wagon to a more pleasing load.

Patent medicine peddlers said that covered bridges hid the view of a town until it was too late to turn back, and certainly one could not turn a horse and wagon around in a covered bridge.

A visiting Englishman in the 19th Century asked, in Victorian logic, if covered bridges weren't actually forts in disguise built for defense against the "Red Hostiles."

It has been said that because covered bridges kept the tread planks dry, they were less subject to damage from the sharp calks of horseshoes.

City folks claimed that while farmers couldn't build a bridge, they did know how to build a barn, hence they combined the two.

Falsely, people often think that bridges were roofed to keep snow off the span. If that were the case, there would be little reason for the abundance of Oregon's covered bridges, since most of them have rarely experienced a severe snowfall.

With a twinkle in his eye, grandfather may have suggested that he stole countless kisses inside a covered "kissing bridge." Although there was only one bridge actually called the "Kissing Bridge," many young suitors took the opportunity of collecting the toll of a kiss upon entering a covered bridge.

The Elkton Bridge: A horse drawn hay wagon passing through the Elk Creek Bridge at Elkton is suggestive of a slower-paced lifestyle. This photo, taken around 1900, shows one of Douglas County's numerous Smith truss structures.

Photo: Douglas County Museum

HOW IT ALL BEGAN

Although few bridges were built in the Oregon Country before the massive migrations of the 1840s, written references give scanty information about them.

Small streams were generally crossed by short open bridges while drift ferries were situated at strategic points along rivers such as the Tualatin, Willamette, Santiam, and Calapooia.

Many counties were content to license ferry operators rather than build bridges. Such franchises were often granted as payment for political debts, creating a monopoly for the transportation of people and goods.

Nels Roney, one of the important bridge builders in Oregon, commented that "the cost of keeping men employed as ferrymen is much more than the interest on the money that will be expended on the building of bridges, and there are many times in the year when ferries are impractical to operate on account of high water."

The matter of transportation was of such concern to Oregon's Provisional Government (1842-1859) that it commanded the attention of the legislature. The Act of December 19, 1845, was the first of many legal aids to encourage private bridge construction. Under this act, the Clackamas Bridge Company was incorporated and later constructed a span known as the "Fendal Cason Bridge" across the Clackamas River.

Along with establishing a minimal bridge width of 12 feet, the act also established toll rates:

For every wagon and a single yoke of oxen or
span of horses, mules, etc. . . . . 25 cents
For a single horse and carriage . . . . 18 cents
For a single footman . . . . 5 cents
For a man and a horse . . . . 10 cents
For all other horses and cattle, per head . . . . . . 3 cents

Enough concern for safe and efficient passage across rivers caused the Provisional Government to authorize the construction of bridges under the auspices of county governments. The provisions of that act, passed September, 1849, stipulated that if 20 or more resident "householders" presented a petition for a bridge, the county was obliged to consider whether the bridge would benefit the public. Each probate court was responsible for raising funds for the construction of bridges and repairs within its jurisdiction. This bill also empowered the county to appoint a bridge commissioner to oversee the construction of bridges who could, ". . . take, or cause to be taken from the adjoining or most convenient lands, such quantity of rock and timber as may be necessary for the building or repairing of such bridge." Landowners furnishing such building supplies were to be amply compensated by the probate court.

Other legislation regarding bridges was passed in the ensuing years, including the establishment of penalties for individuals who ". . . willfully and maliciously cut down or destroy any private, public or toll bridge." In 1851, the legislature fixed the width of all bridges in the territory at no less than 16 feet.

Legislation authorized the incorporation of several companies to build and maintain bridges for profit. Laws regulated tolls, required that income and expenses be recorded for accounting and allowed companies to amortize their debts. However, in actual practice, the tolls varied with the whims of the collector. W. L. Adams, editor of the *Oregon Argus,* reported an experience of his in 1856:

"In crossing a toll bridge on Pudding River this week, kept by Mr. Oakley, we were allowed to pass 'free.' Mr. Oakley said he never charged editors, but like the barber that shaved Greeley, he intended 'to make it up off gentlemen.' "

In later years, as county governments became stronger, they built their own toll-free bridges and public roads funded through taxes collected by the county court. Profit-making spans began to disappear as politicians made a campaign on who would "free" the local bridge. Bond issues and taxation on property values were most often used to finance the construction and maintenance of both bridges and roads.

Many counties, however, were content to franchise a system of toll bridges and toll ferries because in this way, probate courts were not directly responsible for collecting additional taxes and replacing bridges.

Bridge tolls reflected the gains and losses of the local economy. In later years, fees were generally high enough to pocket a modest profit and keep it in repair, but low enough to keep the local voters from wanting to support public bridges with tax dollars.

OREGON'S FIRST COVERED BRIDGE

It is possible that the first covered bridge in Oregon was built by Felix Hathaway in 1850 under the direction of the probate court of Washington County.

Hathaway, a ship's carpenter was a survivor of the wreck of the *William and Ann* which ran aground at the mouth of the Columbia River in March, 1829. Hathaway was the initial master carpenter in the building of the vessel *Star of Oregon* which was sailed to San Francisco in 1841 by a contingent of Oregon farmers. The ship was traded for 350 head of cattle which were driven to the Willamette Valley the next year.

A contract, dated May 8, 1850, and filed with the probate court, described the conditions under which the bridge "across the Tuality River near Hillsbourough" was to be built:

"The string pieces to be four feet above high water mark when bridge is completed. The bridge to be fourteen feet wide and including the aprons, one hundred and fifty feet long—and to be fifty feet between the bents across the main channel of the river . . . the whole to be covered with good two inch plank and completed by the first of September A.D. 1850."

Upon completion of the bridge, the court was to award $1,200 to Hathaway and Alexander Zachary, his financial backer. Unfortunately, county records which might verify the completion of the bridge have been lost over the years, so there is no way to determine if money was paid to Hathaway for the contract.

Hathaway's bridge may have been an uncovered span. An additional provision of the contract provided that:

". . .the construction and workmanship of that part of the bridge between and including the main bents to correspond with the Bridge between Oregon City and the Island in the Willamette River."

This Island Mills Bridge, built in 1847, spanned the Willamette River between the Island Mills and Oregon City. Little is known of it. It probably was not covered. Its replacement, built in 1851, provides the earliest published reference to a covered bridge in the *Oregon Spectator* Oct. 4, 1851: ". . . and for the old bridge to the Island Mills, a new one is in the course of construction." On Nov. 4, confirmation was given that it was to be covered.

Other reports of covered bridges built during the 1850s are somewhat sparse. Nearly every bridge constructed in that era was washed out during the disasterous flood of 1861.

It is likely that Marion County's first covered bridge replaced the flimsy open structure crossing Pringle Creek in South Salem. Daniel Clark and John H. Hayden contracted to build the 200-foot span for $7,500. The *Stateman* editorialized in September, 1862: ". . . although the builders do not feel ashamed of their work, they are busily engaged in covering it." This bridge withstood the flood of 1890 and was replaced shortly thereafter with a steel span.

By the mid-1860s, the idea of covering bridges was fairly well accepted. A Marion County bid notice in 1865 gave the county an option: "All bidders are requested to put in a bid for the bridge, and with and without a roof." The best arguments against the extra cost of covering bridges was their high mortality due to floods and freshets which decreased a useful life from 40 years to no more than 15 years.

The Pringle Creek Bridge (1862). *One of the first photographs of a covered bridge in Oregon shows the Pringle Creek Bridge in Salem. This view was recorded by Wiley Kenyon, Salem's mayor and an amateur photographer, shortly after the structure was completed in 1862. The span survived the flood of 1890 and was replaced in 1892.*

Photo: Salem Public Library, Maxwell Collection

TRUSSES: THE WHAT AND HOWE OF IT

A covered bridge is more than a barn across a stream. It is an engineering marvel, obtaining as much strength with as little material as possible, a triumph expressed in designs representing both time and space.

The concept of a covered bridge was probably first made operational in China as much as 2,000 years ago. The first covered span to be readily identified was built over the Euphrates River near Babylon about 750 B.C.

Prior to the Renaissance, bridges were constructed of stone or were a series of planks on wooden pilings.

In the late 1500s, the Italian architect Andrea Palladio produced a revolutionary design for strengthening a bridge by scientifically arranging triangles of wood to share the strain of the bridge members—thus the truss, one of the most important contributions of the Renaissance period, was invented.

Palladio noted that truss bridges were economical to build, capable of spanning great lengths and were adaptable to the use of short pieces of timber.

Palladio proved the validity of his truss principles by putting together a few kingpost and queenpost wooden truss bridges.

The basic kingpost truss consists of a center upright post framed into a triangle formed by the two diagonals and the bottom chord, or longitudinal member. As all three timbers are in compression, the stress is shared and heavy loads can be accommodated. An example of this type of truss can be found in the Neal Lane Bridge in Douglas County, the only kingpost highway bridge in Oregon.

An early attempt to diminish the size of long diagonal kingpost members was the introduction of a modification in design, called the queenpost. The queenpost truss is an extended kingpost, generally with two uprights instead of one, connected by an upper chord. Four examples of the queenpost truss can be found in Oregon: North Fork Yachats River (Lincoln County), Wimer, Antelope Creek and Lost Creek Bridges (all Jackson County). In the latter three bridges, modifications have been made to the queenpost to strengthen the truss.

The coming of the railroad to America in 1830, heightened the demand for stronger bridges. Seeing a ready market for their patents, carpenters and engineers sought to strengthen earlier designs. One such man was William Howe, a relative of Elias Howe, inventor of the lock-stitch sewing machine.

The distinctive feature of the Howe truss, developed in 1840, was the adoption of iron stress rods to give support to the wooden truss members. Threaded rods with bolts on both ends, could be adjusted to tighten the critical bridge truss joints. Popular with both highway and railroad engineers, the Howe design became the preferred truss as it increased not only the load bearing capacity, but also the life expectancy of the span. The adoption of the Howe truss in Oregon came quickly in the bridge rebuilding program following the flood of 1881. The majority of the extant covered bridges in Oregon are of the Howe design.

The last major effort to improve truss designs was made by Robert W. Smith of Tippecanoe, Ohio, in 1867. The Smith truss was simply a series of diagonal struts placed in an "X" position secured to the top and bottom chords. Termed a "half lattice" truss, the Smith truss was strong, light and cheap to construct. For a number of years the Smith truss dominated bridge design in Oregon though no examples of this type remain.

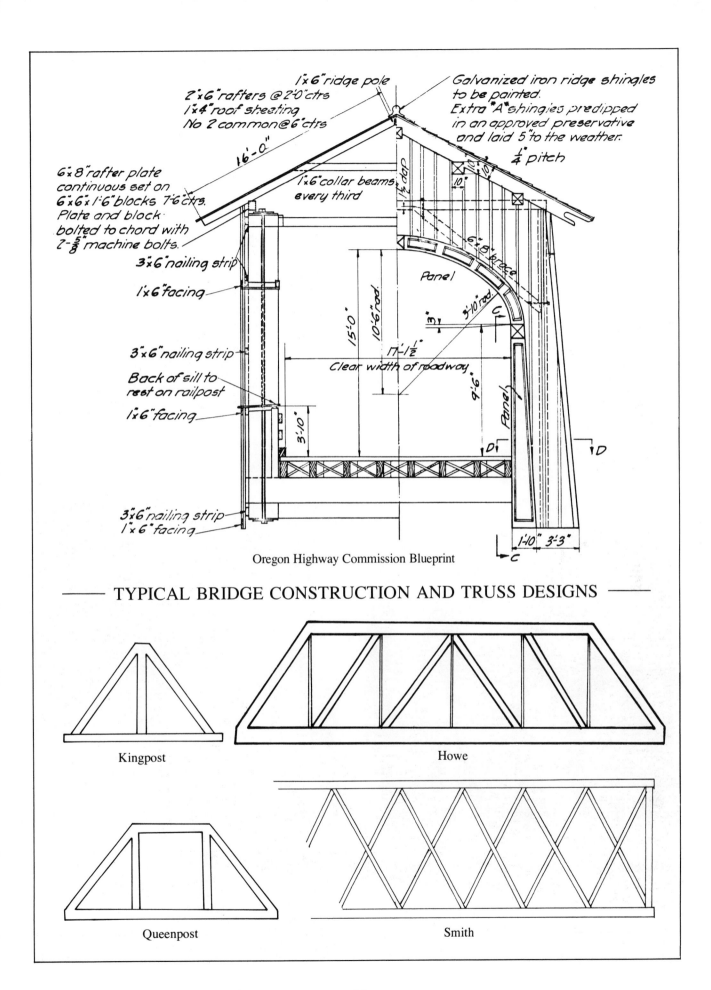

Oregon Highway Commission Blueprint

— TYPICAL BRIDGE CONSTRUCTION AND TRUSS DESIGNS —

Kingpost

Howe

Queenpost

Smith

The Office Bridge Interior. *An interior view of the Office Bridge at Westfir demonstrates the arrangement of wooden members of the Howe truss. The herculean proportions of the timbers readily handles the weight of loaded log trucks which must pass through the bridge. To maintain compression of the truss members, double sets of metal tension rods are used at each panel of the truss.*

The Cooper Bridge. *This interior view of the Cooper Bridge illustrates the placement of timbers of the Smith truss. The covered structure was located across the North Fork of the Coquille River near Myrtle Point. Although the date of the construction is uncertain, the bridge, which consisted of double Smith trusses of 130 and 90 feet, placed end to end and supported by a pier, was built between 1890 and 1908. The span was rebuilt in 1922 and lasted until the 1950s. Distinctive features of the bridge were a curved wooden approach and double spans.*

Photo: Oregon Highway Commission

OREGON'S PROLIFIC BRIDGE BUILDERS

A. S. Miller

Although many competent bridge builders constructed bridges in Oregon, the presence and expertise of two was most highly felt.

One of the most active and prominent bridge builders in the 1870s was Albert S. Miller, of the firm of A. S. Miller and Sons.

Miller had emigrated west from Ohio where he probably became acquainted with Robert Smith's patented bridge truss.

Miller had purchased a franchise for exclusive rights to use the Smith patent in either Oregon or the Washington Territory. Miller's achievements and the strength of the Smith truss were admired by the citizens of the Willamette Valley.

The first Oregon bridge built by A. S. Miller and Sons replaced the Clackamas river Bridge washed out in April, 1872, known as the Fendal C. Cason Bridge. Miller's 1873 contract was for $5,205. The Miller-built truss was five feet longer than that in the proposed design, with a clear span of 215 feet. The total length, including approaches, equalled 356 feet. Supports for the truss were constructed in crib-fashion out of timbers and filled with stone. The bridge was completed in October, 1873, and was hailed as the longest in the state. It was remarkable in that the truss dimensions, 22 feet high by 22 feet wide, were much larger than the minimum sixteen foot width required by law. Miller's company completed many other bridges in Oregon during the 1870s and 1880s. Among those built were the "Spores Ferry" Bridge across the McKenzie, the Knight's Bridge spanning the Molalla River, the Springfield and Eugene City Bridges over the Willamette, several bridges across the South Santiam and two bridges on the Grande Ronde River in Union County. In the early 1880s, the firm contracted for railroad bridges and trestles when the main line was extended south from Roseburg.

Miller retired from the business around 1885. Leadership in bridge building passed to the Portland office of the California-based Pacific Bridge Company.

Shortly after Miller's retirement, bridge building underwent a change heightened by the 1890 flood, to open steel construction, the adoption of shorter Howe truss spans and a more competitive construction market.

The Knight's Bridge. *The Knight's Bridge, named for Joseph Knight, a settler of the Oregon City area, was built by A. S. Miller in 1877 for $4,400. Clackamas County demanded that the Smith truss, so widely used by Miller, not be allowed. A. J. Cason was appointed to supervise the construction and he requested that his own truss design be used. The bridge featured a 87-foot Howe truss and a 123-foot straight "archbrace" truss. The portals of Knight's Bridge were so small that hay loads had to be reduced to pass through the bridge. Wheels often were removed so that machines could be dragged through on the decking. The structure had been condemned to traffic and its siding had been removed when it was blown into the Molalla River in 1947.*

Photo: Salem Public Library, Ben Maxwell Collection

Nels Roney

Among the carpenters working on A. S. Miller's Eugene Bridge in 1876 was a young man who later became one of the most prolific bridge builders in Oregon. Lord Nelson "Nels" Roney came to Oregon from Ohio about 1875 and acquired his bridge building skill while working with Miller. In 1880, he was head carpenter for Miller, building the Gazley Bridge near Canyonville on the Umpqua River in southern Oregon. President Rutherford B. Hayes, on a tour of the west, passed by the Gazley Bridge site and shook hands with Roney and his crew.

The flood of 1881 gave Roney a chance to bid against his former employer in the reconstruction of bridges. Possessing a shrewd business sense, Roney successfully underbid competitors on all phases of bridge construction. He dominated bridge building in Lane County for 20 years.

Roney infrequently deviated from employing the Howe truss, refusing to construct the spans to daring lengths that could weaken the structure. He standardized portal designs, following those adopted by A. S. Miller; these designs identify Lane County bridges.

Roney's bridges gave many years of good service. That may have been due to the conservative length and truss design, but was also due to sound construction techniques. One of Roney's structures lasted 63 years; the average life of the nearly 100 bridges he built was 33 years.

By the end of the century, bridge construction involved a large portion of county budgets. Lane County's budget included only $119.64 for bridge construction in 1872, seventeenth in a list of 25 items. By 1875, bridge costs had risen to first rank in the amount of $9,592.95. In 1891, the amount had increased to $65,553.54, more than half the county's budget. Included in the budget were amounts for replacement of bridges destroyed by flood, and those considered unsafe, as well as maintenance on existing bridges.

Covered bridge building reached a "stagnation point" near the turn of the century. Many of the bridges washed out in the 1890 flood were replaced with steel bridges which offered a potentially more solid roadway.

The Lowell Bridge: *L. N. Roney constructed the 190-foot Howe truss covered bridge across the Middle Fork of the Willamette River near Lowell in 1907. Roney's bridge replaced a ferry at this site which had been operated by Amos Hyland since 1874. Bridges constructed by Roney were built to last. The Lowell Bridge endured 37 years, slightly longer than the average life of the nearly 100 spans he built during his 30 years of bridge construction.*

Photo: Lane County Pioneer Museum

ROOFS OVER RAILS

Early railroad bridge builders who used wood exclusively saw their efforts collapse, wash out and catch fire. In an attempt to construct a bridge to withstand increasingly heavier loads, architects and builders turned to steel as reinforcement. In Oregon, the Howe truss, a combination of wood and steel, was used to carry heavy loads of rolling stock and cargo. The Howe truss was used because it was cheaper and easier to construct than an all wood span.

Other covered railroad bridges were built in succession, including a "combination iron and wood bridge" near Dallas in 1880 which successfully withstood the flood of 1881 while many other bridges were washed out, especially on the Umpqua, Willamette, McKenzie and Santiam Rivers. Most railroad bridge engineers advised rebuilding with a combination iron and wood bridge.

Not all railroad bridges were used solely by trains pulling payloads of cargo and passengers. A notation in Lane County's bridge record in early 1917 was made by bridge inspector J. W. McArthur regarding a bridge over the Row River:

> "Bridge is used by trains and county traffic and since no county road traffic can be on the bridge when the train is, the bridge will be safe for all county purposes whenever it is safe for railroad use. No detailed inspection made, but informed by foreman of the Bohemia Lumber Company's mill that the bridge was tightened up and gone over by the railroad people about a month ago."

Roofs over rails construction continued into the 1930s. The last such bridges to be used were those built for the Smith-Powers Logging Company in the 1920s. The railroad line was extended from Marshfield (now Coos Bay) to Myrtle Point in 1915, and shortly thereafter to Powers. The Smith-Powers Company was purchased by the Georgia-Pacific Corporation which replaced the six covered spans on the Myrtle Creek-Powers section of the railroad in the late 1960s. Salmon Creek Bridge at Powers was converted to truck use until it was closed in the mid-1960s. School children used it as a foot bridge until it was declared totally unsafe. It was removed in September, 1976.

A covered railroad bridge was used on the Springfield-Mohawk line operated by the Weyerhauser Corporation. Built in 1911, the span endured until the 1964 Christmas flood washed it from its abutments.

Only the Chambers Railroad Bridge stands as a reminder of the era in which steam locomotives puffed through wooden "tunnels" across Oregon's streams.

The Broadbent Bridge. *Rebuilding after the 1881 flood, most railroad engineers preferred the Howe truss, or "combination wood and iron bridge" because of the strength afforded by the truss. By the time that the Broadbent Bridge in Coos County was built in 1923, virtually all railroad bridges were of the Howe design. The bridge, and five others along the rail line, were built by the Southern Pacific Railroad linking Powers and Myrtle Point. The span was washed out in 1964 and other covered spans along the line were replaced.*

Photo: Oregon Highway Commission

The Salmon Creek Bridge. *This relic was one of the few covered spans built for rail use and later modified for truck traffic. Built in 1923 by the Smith-Powers Logging operations, the structure carried a frequent payload of timber to a nearby mill until the rail line was removed. Still in good condition, the bridge was converted to truck use about 1960. The span was declared unsafe in the mid-1960s and it was finally pulled down in 1976.*

The Brownsville Bridge. Shortly after the turn of the century, the number of covered bridges in the State began to decline rapidly as open steel bridges began to replace them. This trend continued until the demand for steel during World War I caused a resurgence in the construction of housed wooden spans. Many "iron-pin" and steel bridges built to take the place of covered spans were little better than the structures they replaced. Although the bridges were narrow, they shook under the weight of passing traffic. To alleviate the problem, bridges such as this one over the Calapooia River at Brownsville carried the warnings of a fine for heavy loads.

Photo: Oregon Historical Society

THE BEGINNING OF THE END

Unfortunately, it was the availability of steel that brought about the decline of covered bridges. While the wooden bridges required frequent maintenance, were washed out in nearly every flood, and were expensive to rebuild, iron and steel bridges required little maintenance and, due to the openness of their construction, were not as apt to be washed out.

Sharp-talking bridge salesmen used all of their tricks to convince county courts that wooden bridges were dangerous, and therefore, must be replaced. Wholesale destruction of wooden bridges followed, replaced by iron pin bridges "hawked" for a substantial profit.

In 1915, one of the first actions of the newly formed Oregon State Highway Commission was the investigation of bridge construction. The conclusion of the investigation was that many county courts were being "victimized." In answer, the Highway Commission proposed the enactment of legislation "requiring all bridges costing $500 or more to be built under the direct supervision of the Highway Department."

In 1916, the Highway Commission published a manual on bridge specifications and designs. Basically the manual was designed to help the counties in contracting for bridge construction. In regard to wooden bridges, the praise was high:

"No discussion of bridge work for Oregon county roads would be complete without a fair presentation for the merits of Howe truss bridges covered in (sic). It is because they are now and will continue to be an important element in the development of economical stream crossings on secondary roads for some time to come, that they demand and should receive consideration."

During the next several years, the Highway Department standarized bridge designs. Plans for bridges, including covered spans, were drawn up in lengths to suit any creek or river, and the designs were made available for county to produce a better bridge at less cost to the county.

Many improvements were made as a functional element. Major objections to the continued use of housed spans were summarized in the Highway Commission's Bridge Manual:

"Against the disadvantages which have been mentioned should be considered the greater fire risks, difficulty sometimes in getting teams to cross the dark covered bridges at night and the danger of accidents to teams, or especially automobiles, if the approaches are

The Taft Covered Bridge. In 1924, the U.S. Bureau of Public Roads built a covered span over Schooner Creek at Taft on the Oregon Coast. The 100-foot Howe truss span cost $22,770, including pilings and approaches. This view shows the bridge before the portals were rebuilt in 1943 in a hexagonal shape to provide 14-foot vertical clearance. The bridge was replaced in 1945 by a concrete span. Construction of the Taft Bridge and other bridges within the next several years was an important phase of the Oregon Coast Highway which was completed to the California border in 1932.

Photo: Oregon Historical Society

not on a straight line with the bridge some distance away. The appearance can be improved considerably over that of some bridges now in existence, at very little additional cost."

In 1918, two spans on the Umpqua River near Dillard engineered by the Highway Department, became forerunners to a new architectural style for covered bridges.

Architectural plans for bridges were provided free by the Highway Department and such plans were adopted, for the most part, by the counties with little modification in structural design.

Even during the 1920s, with post-war prosperity and technological advances, the covered bridge proved more economical for many applications than concrete or steel spans. County courts were adamantly cost conscious in approving bridge and road designs.

Often counties constructed unhoused truss bridges and covered them in later years, generally because funds for such "frivolous construction" were not available at the time such bridges were built. Most unhoused wooden spans were covered within two years of their construction as county engineers felt that it was unwise to leave them standing exposed to the weather for longer periods of time.

As early as 1865, notices to bridge contractors provided for bids to be submitted—both with and without a roof. Irate taxpayers expressed divergent views of covering bridge trusses. While some citizens felt the extra cost of roofing a bridge was an unnecessary expense, others filed petitions to house wooden spans in an effort to protect their investment.

Tradition, in part, continued the construction of covered spans during the middle 1920s. The economic condition of the 1930s again called attention to covered bridges as county courts sought a resolution to the problem of constructing and maintaining bridges as county coffers dwindled. Only a few bridges were built in the 1940 era. These generally were financed by county courts and reflected the conversion of steel use to the war effort.

In the last several decades, only a few covered spans have been initiated. Two of these, Milo Academy and Rock O' the Range, are privately owned.

It appears that the days of covered bridge construction may be over. Costs of materials, labor and maintenance render such structures impractical. Additionally, increasing traffic and load limits dictate weight capacities beyond those of which most covered spans were designed to carry.

In the last 15 years, the number of covered bridges in Oregon has decreased by almost 50 percent. While several of these were washed away or destroyed in the flood of 1964, most have fallen victim to progress.

The John Day River Bridge. *The demand for steel during World War I led the Oregon State Highway Commission to overcome its objection to wooden covered spans in the construction of the John Day River Bridge east of Astoria. Since the main objection was the lack of light in roofed structures, bridge engineers included windows between upright truss members and specified that the interior be whitewashed. Built to handle 20-ton trucks, the bridge cost the state about $25,000, partly because of the uniqueness of the construction. A 40-foot counterweighted draw span between two 108-foot Howe truss main spans allowed passage of river traffic. The bridge was replaced in 1933 after 15 years of service.*

Photo: Oregon Highway Commission

The Ritner Creek Bridge. *By 1927, when the Ritner Creek Bridge was built, the State Highway Department had supplied considerable technical information on bridges to county road departments. Generally, such information was in the form of bridge designs, including blueprints for the truss, bents, roof and siding. Occasionally the Highway Department would assist the counties in aspects of civil engineering and in readying bids. Some counties, notably Lane and Linn, often used truss designs furnished by the state, but supplied their own designs for the housings.*

Photo: Salem Public Library, Maxwell Collection

FLOODS, FIRES AND OTHER MALADIES

Freshets and Floods

Prior to the turn of the century, high water and flooding constantly caused deep concern to the bridge designer and builder. Major floodings enabled Oregon bridge builders to remain employed, replacing bridges that washed away. Catastrophic flooding occurred in 1853, 1861, 1881, and 1890. These rampaging floods carried dozens of the covered structures downstream to destruction. Often a bridge upstream collided with one downstream, creating a devastating, floating bridge-jam. Floods have periodically destroyed bridges, from the earliest flooding recorded in Oregon history, up to the last major flooding in 1964.

Historians have written that the winter of 1861-1862 was the most severe in Oregon history. A cold fall had produced deep snows and these were followed by warm rains, forming torrents from the mountains. When the mountain run-off met the half-melted snow in the valley, it formed a mass of heavy slush which was unable to push its way through the gorge at Oregon City. According to Historian John Horner:

". . . the swollen tide of back-water spread over the valley to such depth that settlers said that an ocean liner could have sailed over some of their farms. Many actually tasted the water to tell whether the sea had broken through its mountain barrier."

The flooding waters washed clean the banks of both sides of the Willamette, both below and above Willamette Falls at Oregon City, and inundated the entire Willamette Valley. It destroyed mills, stores, hotels, a machine shop, a warehouse, and every building near the falls. The flood provided a situation that has never been equalled, when on December 5, 1861, Captain S. R. Smith and Engineer

---

The Eugene City Bridge. *High waters of the 1890 flood carried away nearly all of the major covered wooden bridges within the Oregon boundaries. The Willamette River at Eugene destroyed the north approach in early February. Rebuilding of the span was soon completed by Nels Roney, and the total length exceeded 350 feet.*

Photo: Lane County Pioneer Museum

14730

Flood of Feb 4th, '90

Alonzo Vickers brought the steam ship *St. Clair* over the falls close to the Oregon City side. Below the falls, the river had risen 75 feet.

Just 20 years later, the 1881 flood removed most of the covered bridges in the Willamette Valley. Lane County suffered the loss of the newly built Springfield and Eugene covered bridges.

The 1890 flood was even more devastating to Oregon's covered bridges, as nearly every large bridge in the Willamette Valley was washed downstream. The Eugene City covered bridge lost a newly added span and the north approach, but the main span remained. The rebuilding of the

replacement span and approach was awarded to Nels Roney. When finished, the two spans totalled 350 feet, and travelers must have been confused over the identity of the bridge builder. The boldly lettered sign over the portal of the north span stated, "Built by L. N. Roney," while travelers going the opposite direction could read, "Built by A. S. Miller."

Other losses over the years were severe, including the 1964 Christmas flood that forced near panic in the western part of the state. High water reduced the bridge population in Lane County by washing three of that county's covered spans downstream into oblivion. Flooding waters of the McKenzie removed the 27-year-old Belknap Bridge from existence, while on the Coast Fork of the Willamette, the Rouse Bridge was damaged to the extent it had to be replaced. A third bridge to be removed by the flood waters was Lane County's last operating railroad bridge which crossed the Mohawk River a mile north of Hayden Bridge. Another bridge damaged during the 1964 Christmas flood was the Stewart Bridge, five miles south of Cottage Grove over Mosby Creek. The cracked lower chords were replaced and the bridge is still in use. Flood waters also removed the Menthorne Bridge in Jackson County as well as several covered railroad spans in Coos County.

The Pringle Creek Bridge. Salem's first covered bridge over Pringle Creek survived the flood of 1890, even though high water lapped at its underpinnings. City fathers considered the covered span to be a hinderance to progress and were elated when it was replaced in 1892 with an open steel span. It was said that filth which accumulated within the bridge never seemed to get cleaned out, and that unlighted covered "barns" such as this were "convenient places for tramps and holdups."
Photo: Salem Public Library, Ben Maxwell Collection

Gales, Gusts . . . and Gone

Often the design and construction of the covered bridge resulted in presenting a clumsy attempt to span the waters. The covered structure, barn-like in appearance, actually had a "box-kite" effect in high winds and many of these bridges were actually blown from their pilings and abutments. Bridges often developed a swaying motion from strong, whipping winds and buttresses were added to strengthen the bridge to make it more rigid, to eliminate this defect. Cross-bracing of the roof saved many a bridge from a watery grave.

Attempts were made to minimize the resistance of covered spans to the effect of winds. The lofty Wallace Bridge, joining Polk and Yamhill Counties, featured twelve windows on each side. This unusual fenestration allowed the ferocious winds of the Yamhill River gorge to gust through the covered bridge without damaging the structure. After the Wallace Bridge was by-passed in 1935, the siding and roof were removed and it served as a foot bridge until it was blown into the Yamhill River in the early 1940s.

The famous Columbus Day storm of October 12, 1962, helped to hasten the replacement of at least two roofed spans. One of these was replaced with another covered bridge, the rebuilt Shimanek covered structure in Linn County near Scio. Trees blown against the bridge damaged it so badly that the roof had to be dismantled and the load limit was lowered to two tons. The damaged structure served the the area in that limited capacity until it was rebuilt in 1966. Another bridge replaced by damage incurred by the October 12 storm was the bridge at Hoskins in Benton County. A large tree was blown onto the structure, damaging the truss members so extensively that it could not be repaired, causing a concrete span to be built at the site.

Excessive wind pressure was a factor encouraging the State Highway Department to approve designs of exposed trusses so widely used in Linn County. This practice not only increased visibility and lighting, but also reduced the tremendous thrusts generated by wind storms.

Snow: Drifts and Destruction

Unlike many of the covered bridges in the northeastern portion of the United States, most of the Oregon covered bridges rarely have snowy roofs. It has been a long standing myth that snowfall was one of the reasons for covering bridge trusses in Oregon. However, a periodic snowfall does cause trouble, and sometimes damages the roof or structure of the bridges.

Heavy snows proved the worst enemy of covered bridges in 1943 and 1969. Early in 1943, the bridge across the Sandy River near Zig Zag was crushed under the weight of the winter snow storm and fell into the river. The snowfall of 1969 was equally detrimental. It brought snow levels to such depths that bridge roofs collapsed under the weight. The Pass Creek Bridge at Drain was so damaged that crews had to repair the remaining portions of the bridge. Worried residents were placated only when they discovered that the workmen were repairing the structure and not dismantling it.

Roof damage also was a result of the 1969 snowstorm at the Lower Portage Bridge spanning the North Fork of the Siuslaw River. The roof was removed and the structure was used in the uncovered condition until its destruction one year later. The bridge had been scheduled for replacement in 1970.

Two other covered spans suffered extensive damage from the heavy snows of that storm. The roof of the Coyote Creek Bridge in Lane County collapsed under three feet of snow.

The Roaring Camp covered bridge in Douglas County received a new roof as a result of the January snows and other repairs were made while the workmen were at the bridge site.

The Saginaw Bridge. A Ford Model A is shown emerging from the Saginaw Bridge built during 1943-44. This 165-foot span cost Lane County $19,055. The original covered span was built in 1883 featuring an unusual truss combination. A 143-foot covered Howe truss and a 41-foot open queenpost truss spanned the Coast Fork of the Willamette River just north of Cottage Grove. The replacement span endured until high water damaged the structure in December 1964. The damage, as well as the demands of traffic on Highway 99, caused the bridge to be replaced by a concrete span.
Photo: Lane County Pioneer Museum

The Wallace Bridge. The 115-foot Wallace Bridge, crossing the South Yamhill river, between Buell and Valley Junction in Polk County, was built in 1919 by Earl C. Bushnell. Bushnell used timbers 120 feet in length, 14" x 16" for the bottom chords of the trusses. The twelve windows on each side reduced the force of wind gusts and lighted the bridge interior. The structure was used until it was by-passed in 1935 with a steel and concrete span. The old wooden bridge was left standing, but the covering had been removed to reduce the dead weight. Polk County survey crews used the uncovered structure as a foot bridge until the early 1940s, when strong winds blew it into the river.
Photo: Salem Public Library, Ben Maxwell Collection

Tinder Boxes

The wooden truss members, bracing and flooring under the bridge covering dried with age and became covered with dust form the passage of years of use. The dry timber could ignited into a ball of flame with only a spark, as early bridge timbers were not treated with fire retardent materials. Counties reported that most bridge fires were the result of negligence and carelessness and warnings of "no smoking" were posted on many bridge portals.

The roof covering on railroad bridges was often ignited from the smoking debris from the coal burning steam locomotives. Railroads hired watchmen to look for sparks and embers which belched from passing trains. Shortly thereafter, an ingenious workman devised a way to install water barrels on the roofs to act as an automatic sprinkling system.

Although legislation has protected the covered bridges from vandalism since the early 1850s, even recently misguided persons have attempted to burn covered bridges, believing they were doing a service in removing a public hazard. Charred timbers on the Chambers Railroad Bridge at Cottage Grove gives evidence to attempts of this type. Planks in the deck flooring of both the Upper Drift Creek and Horse Creek Bridges were recently blackened either by vandals or uninformed picnickers.

Benton County employees soon discovered public scorn after burning a by-passed covered bridge over the Long Tom River. County crews put torches to the 50-year-old Bundy Bridge after it had developed a sag of almost five feet when its pilings rotted. Likewise, in Jackson County, officials decided that the Yankee Creek covered bridge had outlived it usefulness. Crews dismantled the bridge and burned the remains in piles beside the new replacement. A caption in the *Oregonian* reflected the feelings of many of Jackson County's residents, "Embers smoldered and so did

The Brownsville Rail Bridge. This stylish railroad span across the Calapooya River at Brownsville was built about 1890 by Hoffman and Bates. It is identical to a Hoffman and Bates bridge that crossed Thomas Creek near Scio. In an attempt to provide an early day automatic sprinkling system, barrels of water were placed on the roof. Additional barrels of water were located on the approaches in the event that sparks should ignite the shingled exterior. Hoffman and Bates bridges used the slant of the end diagonal truss members to eliminate unnecessary framework squaring the portals. Flying buttresses added strength to the structure and the large eave overhang protected the siding. The rail line, built by the Oregon and California Railroad, was acquired by Southern Pacific who gave it the name, "Road to a Thousand Wonders." Like other covered railroad spans on the rail line, the Brownsville bridge was replaced about 1920.

Photo: Oregon Historical Society

tempers, as the timbers were burned in two bridgeside bon-fires."

Aside from educating the public of the possible hazard of fires destroying covered bridges, only defensive tactics of treating the timbers, applying fire retardant paint, and as-phalting the flooring are realistic preventatives.

Warnings and Regulations

Long life for the covered bridge has always been a concern of the bridge users, toll collectors, as well as the bridge designers. The first corrective action was brought forth by the toll-takers because these individuals felt that heavy loads shortened the lives of the bridges. They charged a greater toll for loaded wagons and buggies, and extra if the size and weight warranted.

The early Oregon bridges had warnings posted, threaten-ing a fine for offenders of speed or weight violations. Such warnings included hand scrawled signs such as the one posted on one western bridge:

NOTIS
"No veahcle drawn by moar than one animile
is aloud to cros this Bridg in opposite direxions
at the sam Time."

During the heyday of the horse and buggy era, signs over the arches of old wooden covered bridges warned, "Walk Your Horses." Later, the arrival of the automobile forced alterations of the signs to include, "Speed Limit, 10 miles per hour."

The Deadwood Bridge. *This 112-foot Howe truss span was built in 1903 by A. N. Striker over Deadwood Creek near the town of Deadwood in Lane County. It carried the admonition of a $25 fine for riding or driving over it faster than a walk, or for driving more than 10 head of horses or cattle over the bridge at one time.*
Photo: Oregon Historical Society

Legislation enacted prior to 1900 required drivers of traction-driven engines to carry pieces of plank to be used as support in crossing bridges. Until its replacement in the 1960s, the Lincoln County bridge at Harlan had a warning posted, "No Cleated Tractors," and even today, a sign posted on the North Fork Yachats bridge still warns users of this regulation.

Covering a wooden bridge increases the possible life span up to five times of those bridges left uncovered. Likewise, treating the vital truss members and pilings increases the odds of longer utilization. Early builders used brine or salt as a preservative. Later, white lead, tar, or creosote were used. Heat and pressure treatment was one of the latter methods employed to ensure longer life for timber members. However, untreated timbers lasted for years, as was evidenced in a 1929 University of Oregon study. E. H. McAllister salvaged several untreated timbers from two of McKenzie River bridges built in 1874. He found all the timbers to be in sound condition, and indeed, as strong as the steel bridges that replaced them. P. M. Morse, a Lane County engineer and surveyor, explained that timbers gain strength through the years as they season under dry roofs. He reported that they gained about one-half again in strength as when installed.

Early attempts to determine the load capacity of a bridge were limited scientifically. Overweighted loads were prevented from crossing earlier toll bridges by the use of small portal openings, which may have allowed only lighter loads. Not only did that force wagons to carry smaller loads, but mounted riders also had to get off and walk.

The Greenwood Bridge. In 1941, the Greenwood Bridge spanning *Rickreall Creek in Polk County west of Salem suffered irreparable damage when state highway crews hauled asphalt over the old wooden structure. Heavy truck traffic over the bridge caused the weakened structure to collapse, and driver Sam Lowery and his truck fell with the bridge. County crews had removed the roof and siding just prior to the collapse and the replacement had already been scheduled. The practice of removing the roof and siding to reduce the "dead weight" was a common method of extending the bridge life.*
Photo: Salem Public Library, Ben Maxwell Collection

The Umatilla River Bridge. Structural floor bracing of this span *in Pendleton collapsed under the weight of a steam-powered tractor as shown in this 1905 photograph. Many spans had weight restrictions posted and in many cases, drivers of such steam driven engines were required to utilize extra planking for reinforcement when crossing.*
Photo: Oregon Historical Society, Wilson Collection

DANCE HALLS, BILLBOARDS AND HOTELS

The sides and portals of covered bridges were often painted with advertisements or announcements of local color. An upcoming circus or revival meeting usually prompted the promoter to post the billing on a highly travelled landmark, and the community covered bridge was chosen more often than a nearby barn. The tin signs and posters are all but gone today, but the Ernest and Wendling Bridges in Lane County still show traces of circus posters pasted between the truss members.

Community members frequently tacked bulletins and notices in neighboring covered bridges. Portal boarding was usually covered with advertisements and items of interest nailed there by residents in the area. Faster-paced traffic eliminated this practice during the period following the horse and buggy era.

Citizens have recently requested that county bridge superintendents allow them the opportunity to paint murals or designs on covered bridges, but they have been denied as counties want to maintain a uniformity in their bridge colors.

During the early years of the 20th century, map designers used covered bridges as reference points on area maps produced in that period. Motoring guides and bicycle tour books often referred to covered bridge locations as road markers and mile posts.

When the covered bridges were more numerous, discarded or unused structures were sometimes utilized as barns and tool sheds. The Cross Bridge in Tillamook County and the Salado Bridge in Lincoln County were retired to a barn status. The Crawfordsville span was used to house a local resident's log truck until the county installed end railings. Several bridges, including Remote, Ritner Creek, Sam's Creek, and Upper Drift Creek have been bypassed to be used for parks or reminders of their more useful past.

Many of the covered bridges in Oregon provided social gathering places for local residents. The coolness of the passing stream and the roof of the bridge provided protection from the heat of summer. In early Oregon history, political rallies were held in covered bridges because other places were not available, especially since some churches would not allow them to be held there. Poker parties, grange meetings and dances were held in some western Oregon bridges as well.

In the 1860s, the Pringle Creek Bridge in Salem provided a place for an Indian wedding and at least one baby reportedly was born in an Oregon covered bridge. The score, however, is much higher for persons who died in them. Stories are told of highwaymen who hid in the dark shadows of covered bridges to prey on unwary travelers. Jealous lovers also many have waited in the gloomy interior of the covered bridges to ambush a rival.

Many a covered bridge was used for an overnight hotel, but the Swisshome Bridge was involved in an unusual housekeeping incident. Much like the bridges of New England which had been used for camp meetings and drill floors for militia, the Swisshome Bridge also served other purposes. In the 1920s, the Woolsey family from Indian Creek, numbering eleven strong, set up housekeeping and spent the winter in the wooden structure as the roads to their home became impassable. It took a visit by the constable in the spring to evict the stubborn family. While the Woolsey's lived there, travelers who desired to cross the bridge had to wait while family members moved their belongings to the allow traffic to pass.

The Swisshome Bridge. *Nels Roney constructed the original Swisshome covered span in 1887. The bridge cost just $3,875 and lasted until the 1890 flood washed it away. The replacement also built by Roney was a 170-foot Howe truss span costing $5,850 in 1890. It was used until 1919. Lane County rebuilt the structure, at a cost of $8,240 and it was inhabited by the Woolsey family for a winter season. The span, measuring 180 feet in length, endured until 1961, when it was replaced.*

Photo: Lane County Pioneer Museum

The Hagood Bridge. *The Hagood Bridge, built by contractors St. John and Stone in 1895, was one of the two covered spans built in the city of Dallas. But the county court declared that the Hagood covered structure, crossing the La Creole River at North Main Street, was unsafe. A concrete replacement built in 1921, eliminated the last covered bridge in Dallas. Posting of signs, posters, and advertisements was typical on many early community covered bridges. This old wooden structure helped to advertise Enameline Stove Oil. Traffic using the roofed river crossing prior to the advent of the automobile, had time to pause and ponder over the validity of the announcement.*

Photo: Oregon Historical Society

The Little River Bridge. *The bridge spanning Little River near the present Cavitt Creek span provided the back drop for this early 1900 photograph. Participants in horse drawn conveyances were journeying to a July 4th celebration near Glide.*
Photo: Douglas County Museum

THE PASSING OF THE COVERED BRIDGE

The number of covered bridges in Oregon is declining and the causes of this decline are varied. In 1933, 309 covered bridges were listed within the state boundaries. By 1944, the census of bridges revealed a decline to 231 standing bridges. Just 10 years later, in 1954, the bridge population in the state had dropped to 134 and of these, 125 were on county and private roads, one on a state primary highway, and eight on state secondary highways. The inventory of covered bridges in the state by the year 1962 totalled 95. Today, only 56 survive and none of these remains on a state highway.

One of the key factors in determining whether covered bridges would be built or be retained in use was a concern about the costs to be incurred by the counties or the state. Increasing costs for materials and labor accelerated the construction of steel and concrete spans. Since World War II, the price of wood has doubled or tripled, making other materials less expensive. Additionally, the intricate construction of covered spans has dictated systematic inspections and repair of the structures to maintain them is a safe condition. The complexity of timber truss bridges made detection more difficult in assessing the deterioration of wooden truss members, decking, siding, and pilings. The replacement of chords, pilings and bents often required specially cut timbers.

Equally difficult to acquire were the services of a qualified and dedicated bridge repairman. The men who built covered spans are no longer available to repair them. Bridge builders such as George Breeding and A. C. Striker, who constructed bridges in Lane County, Floyd Frear, who engineered covered spans in Douglas County, and Otis Hamer, builder of wooden truss bridges in Benton, Polk and Lincoln counties, have left their legacies in the spans they built.

As we have seen, the majority of covered bridges replaced or destroyed is a decision made by men, not by nature. The list of bridges declared unsafe for modern traffic or too costly to maintain is long and disheartening. During the 1950s, such bridges as the Moody, Bates Park, McKercher, Dickie Prairie, and the Molalla River Bridges were destroyed as being unsafe and too costly to maintain. The Mill Creek covered bridge on the Alsea Highway was declared outdated and dismantled in 1953 after 29 years of service on a state primary highway.

During the 1960s the "slaughtering" of covered bridges continued at a rapid rate. Bridges lost included Bundy, Kiger Island, Philomath and Dodge Slough in Benton County; Mary White and Lower Portage in Lane County; Slick Rock and Harlan in Lincoln County; and Bryant Park in Linn County. Some covered railroad spans in Coos County were demolished, too. A local garden club was unsuccessful in preserving the Philomath Bridge when estimates exceeded $20,000 to ready the crippled bridge for vehicular traffic. It was estimated that $10,000 was needed to install the necessary corrections just to make the bridge safe for foot traffic.

At least one bridge met a better fate. A newspaper reported the results of efforts by volunteers in Jackson County in 1965. "Hundreds of man hours of labor and several thousands of dollars worth of materials have been donated in the project of saving the McKee Covered Bridge."

Already during the 1970s, the covered bridge losses include Mapleton (Lane County), Yankee Creek (Jackson County), and McDonald (Douglas County) as well as the Salmon Creek Railroad Bridge at Powers.

The destruction of the Yankee Creek Bridge became an emotional issue in 1974. The bridge was in a sad state of repair and costs to maintain the weakened structure were high. After the bridge was dismantled and burned, the *Oregonian* noted that the "bridge was jerked down without considering the alternatives."

In contrast, the Lincoln County commissioners reported in 1975 that five covered bridges have been lost since 1963 and called for a meeting of interested individuals to save the six remaining covered bridges. Because of added efforts in that county, care has been taken to ensure proper repair and maintenance to keep the old wooden bridges structurally and aesthetically sound.

Efforts to preserve the state's remaining covered bridges by federal, state, and local groups can be encouraging. Historical societies, interested individuals, state agencies, and newspapers keep hopes alive that the end is not "just around the corner."

The Turner Bridge. The Turner Bridge spanning Mill Creek just east of the Marion County town served the area for nearly 25 years. The wooden structure, built in 1922, lasted until the county replaced it with a modern concrete bridge in 1946. A daily user of the bridge was Ed "Tex" Collins, a colorful character residing in nearby Aumsville. He and his horse, Old Silver, travelled the route daily, visiting farmers and neighbors along the way. Ed always wore the familiar hat, large belt buckle, denim jeans, boots, and winter BVDs in place of a shirt. On this particular ride in 1946, photographer Ben Maxwell persuaded "Tex" to pose for a picture, recording the more popular mode of travel of twenty years earlier.

Photo: Salem Public Library, Ben Maxwell Collection

The Quines Creek Bridge. *Most Oregon covered spans appeared more handsome than the Quines Creek Bridge near Azalea. The 100-foot structure, built in 1913, lasted until the trusses collapsed in 1958. At that time, the bridge was probably Oregon's last example of a Smith truss. By 1954 the structure was struggling to handle daily traffic, and the loads of passing log trucks had splintered boards of both the portal openings.*
Photo: Salem Public Library, Ben Maxwell Collection

The Hoskins Bridge. *The roofed wooden structure at Hoskins met the destructive tools of workmen in 1962. Officials decided that the bridge had reached the end of its practical life when the total costs of repairs were evaluated. A sign posted at the site sadly forewarned users of the final date of service: "This bridge will be out MON 24."*
Photo: Salem Public Library, Ben Maxwell Collection

The Mill Creek Bridge, Benton County. *This structure, spanning Mill Creek near Alsea, was the last covered bridge used on a state primary highway (Ore. 34). The Benton County span, built in 1924, lasted until its replacement in 1953. Like most covered bridges designed by state engineers, modern traffic patterns outdated the Mill Creek Bridge before the end of its useful life was reached.*

Photo: Oregon Highway Commission

The Yankee Creek Bridge. *The dismantling of the Yankee Creek Bridge covered span in the early 1970s reduced Jackson County's bridge numbers to just four. The 42-foot wooden structure, constructed in 1922, was the subject of a-much-heated debate when the county decided to replace it. Most users of the old bridge felt that safety was a deciding factor in its replacement.*

Photo: Oregon Highway Commission

SCARICITY BRINGS HOPE FOR THE REMAINING VESTIGES

As the number of covered bridges dwindles, the people of Oregon are acting to ensure the preservation of the state's remaining bridges. Efforts to maintain the bridges are evident in the recent retirement of the Ritner Creek span near Pedee in Polk County. The decision to build a new concrete bridge was met with favor, but the destruction of the old wooden bridge brought strong opposition from local residents. In addition to letters to editors of newspapers, petitions, and other pressure techniques, citizens tried and succeeded with a more persuasive device—the ballot box. The successful ballot measure provided the funds to move the roofed structure downstream where a park is being established to complement it in its new setting. Covered bridge watchers can enjoy the old bridge safely on foot.

County officials court trouble when they announce the replacement of a covered span. When the proposed replacement of the Weddle Bridge was announced, angry citizens inundated all levels of government from the Linn County engineer to the governor's office. Further study indicated that the bridge could remain intact, and the road rerouted several hundred feet downstream.

Not only should the old wooden spans be saved, they should be maintained in a near-natural setting. The by-pass proposal of the Currin Bridge in Lane County has caused a controversy concerning the location of the new concrete span. Engineers want the new bridge just a few feet away from the old roofed model as little road alignment would be needed. However, covered bridge enthusiasts have recommended that the new span be situated much further away to allow for safety and opportunity for photographic and visual enjoyment.

The majority of Oregon's remaining covered bridges are under county jurisdiction. But, perhaps surprisingly, the major hope for their survival is the protection provided by state and federal legislation. The National Historic Preservation Act of 1966 (Public Law 89-665) established a *National Register of Historic Places,* a voluminous book identifying those buildings, structures, districts, sites, and objects significant in American history, architecture, archeology and culture. Eligibility of the *National Register,* provides a measure of federal protection from adverse effect by federal undertakings, and potential eligibility for some acquisition and restoration funding assistance.

In Oregon, the State Historic Preservation Office in the State Parks and Recreation Branch maintains the *Statewide Inventory of Historic Properties.* A seven-member, governor-appointed State Advisory Committee on Historic Preservation reviews properties in the statewide inventory and recommends to the State Historic Preservation officer those properties that merit nomination to the *National Register.*

For many years the Oregon State Highway Division, through its Bridge Design and Travel Information Sections has maintained a census of covered bridges in the state. Building on the latter work, the State Historic Preservation Office is taking a close look at Oregon's covered bridges to determine their eligibility for the *National Register of Historic Places.* It is hoped that most of the bridges ultimately will be entered into the *Register* under a single, comprehensive Thematic Group nomination. Federal laws do not guarantee the preservation of all covered spans eligible for inclusion in the *Register,* but they do provide for complete

disclosure and evaluation of federally-sponsored plans to destroy or disturb such properties.

Once a covered bridge is bypassed or otherwise removed from any of the federally-supported highway systems, the means of protection lie with the county and the public. Counties are not always able to provide the funding, or in some cases, the motivation for preserving all of the structures within its boundaries. Listing in the *National Register* could, in most cases, facilitate preservation by providing the county with matching funds for accurate restoration.

The initiative for the preservation of covered bridges should not be left entirely to the various government agencies. Some ideas for individuals who want to act toward the preservation of covered bridges are as follows:

1. Become familiar with covered bridges and keep watch for plans to bypass or replace them.
2. Assist the county in obtaining sufficient funding to maintain the covered bridges both on and off the county highway system.
3. Suggest that the local historical society establish covered bridge preservation as a goal and a first order project.
4. Join or organize a "Save the _____ Covered Bridge" campaign.
5. Write letters in support of covered bridges to: Oregon State Historic Preservation Office, State Parks and Recreation Branch, Oregon Highway Division. Your local newspaper, radio stations, county commissioners, legislators, the governor, and your congressmen, any relative or friend who has influence with government officials.
6. Study the environmental impact statement on the project that would destroy the bridge.
7. Testify at public hearings on the bridge project.
8. If all else looks like it is failing, raise some funds and hire a good attorney.
9. If you become desperate, buy the bridge. (Others have!)

In the final analysis, the responsibililty for the preserving the old wood landmarks rest with each of us. We have the opportunity as well as the responsibility to assist in the saving, and if needed, the restoration of these covered structures. In the majority of cases, these efforts of individuals and groups can harmonize with those of the county road departments. Public interest in the preservation of bridges often reaches exciting levels, but the interest wanes when the collection of funds for the project begins. Attitudes such as these can force counties into financial havoc. The total costs of building covered bridges prior to 1940 ranges from $5,000 to $10,000 per bridge, but the repair expense alone on the Linn County Bohemian Hall Bridge exceeded $10,000 in 1975. The average upkeep for repairs to roofs, siding, approaches, and painting exceeds $2,500 per bridge. When the Shimanek Bridge spanning Thomas Creek was rebuilt in 1966, the construction expenses soared to an excess of $60,000 plus additional costs of $6,500 for grading and paving the roadway. Replacement bridges of concrete can be built for about the same cost with no upkeep expense.

The counties have often incurred extra expenses and man hours of labor to provide their citizens these links with the past. We should not forget the inconvenience many counties have sustained in maintaining traffic control as well as the added safety liability caused by some of the weakened bridges. Hopefully, the remaining bridges of Oregon can be enjoyed by our children, our children's children, and . . .

Above: *The technique for notching the upper chord to hold the wooden angle block is featured at the Hoffman Bridge, Linn County.*

Opposite: *Additional years of use can be utilized if counties rebuild and preserve old worn out bridges. The Upper Drift Creek Bridge in Lincoln County is one of that county's three covered spans restricted to "Foot Traffic Only."*

The Goodpasture Bridge Interior. *These Gothic-style windows placed between truss members of the Goodpasture Bridge demonstrate attempts by bridge designers to illuminate the interiors of covered spans. Such fenestration allows an additional architectural dimension to covered bridge construction. Unfortunately, Lane County has made plans to by-pass the Goodpasture Bridge by 1980. Efforts should be made to preserve Oregon's most distinctive and best-known covered bridge.*

COVERED BRIDGE WORLD GUIDE NUMBERING SYSTEM

During the 1950s, a system of identifying covered bridges on a national level was developed by Betsy and Philip Clough and has been adopted by the National Society for the Preservation of Covered Bridges. Local naming of covered spans proved to be inconsistent and many bridges carried several names. Because of bridge name confusion, no accurate national inventory or identification was available until the development of the World Guide numbering system.

Actual assignment of each bridge number is the combination of state, county, and bridge location. Oregon, being the 37th state in the Union alphabetically, dictates the first number of 37 for all roofed spans. Counties too are assigned numbers in alphabetical order. All covered spans in Benton County contain the number 37-02- because that county is second in the state alphabetically. The third set of numbers is assigned to the actual bridge location, although the name of bridge, stream, or township have no factor in the assignment. Since many bridges have been destroyed since the adoption of the World Guide, many numbers are missing, as the numbers are not reused or reassigned.

The Mapleton Bridge. One of Lane County's most beautiful bridges was Mapleton Bridge over the Siuslaw River. A double span with two 105-foot trusses, it was built in six months with Civilian Conservation Corps aid in mid-1934. All four bottom chords, each measuring 16" x 18" x 113' were hand hewn. The length of the bridge, including approaches, totalled 647 feet. The bridge was considered a draw span because the river is navigable to this point but water pipes would have to be disconnected and a crane used to open the drawspan. The Mapleton Bridge was replaced by a concrete span in 1970. Plans to salvage the bridge and use it at a site on the Siletz River failed, and the covered structure was destroyed.

INDEX OF OREGON COVERED BRIDGES

County	World Guide #	Bridge Name	Stream	Year Built	Truss	Pg. No.
Benton	37-02-04	Harris	Mary's River	1936	Howe	8
	37-02-05	Hayden	Alsea River	1918	Howe	9
	37-02-09	Irish Bend	Willamette Slough	1954	Howe	10
Coos	37-06-09	Remote	Sandy Creek	1921	Howe	13
Deschutes	37-09-01	Rock 'o the Range	Swalley Canal	1963	Kingpost	15
Douglas	37-10-02	Pass Creek	Pass Creek	1925	Howe	18
	37-10-04	Rochester	Calapooya R.	1933	Howe	19
	37-10-06	Cavitt Creek	Little River	1943	Howe	20
	37-10-07	Neal Lane	Myrtle Creek	1929	Kingpost	21
	37-10-10	Milo Academy	S. Umpqua R.	1962	Steel	22
	37-10-11	Roaring Camp	Elk Creek	1929	Howe	23
Jackson	37-15-02	Antelope Creek	Antelope Creek	1922	Queenpost	26
	37-15-03	Lost Creek	Lost Creek	1919	Queenpost	27
	37-15-05	Wimer	Evans Creek	1927	Queenpost	28
	37-15-06	McKee	Applegate River	1917	Howe	29
Josephine	37-17-01	Grave Creek	Grave Creek	1920	Howe	31
Lane	37-20-02	Coyote Creek	Coyote Creek	1922	Howe	34
	37-20-04	Wildcat	Wildcat Creek	1925	Howe	35
	37-20-06	Lake Creek	Lake Creek	1928	Howe	36
	37-20-09	Meadows	N. F. Siuslaw R.	1922	Howe	37
	37-20-10	Goodpasture	McKenzie River	1938	Howe	38
	37-20-11	Belnap	McKenzie River	1966	Howe	39
	37-20-12	Horse Creek	Horse Creek	1930	Howe	40
	37-20-15	Pengra	Fall Creek	1938	Howe	41
	37-20-17	Unity	Fall Creek	1936	Howe	42
	37-20-18	Lowell	Md. F. Willamette R.	1945	Howe	43
	37-20-19	Parvin	Lost Creek	1921	Howe	44
	37-20-22	Currin	Row River	1925	Howe	45
	37-20-23	Dorena	Row River	1949	Howe	46
	37-20-27	Mosby Creek	Mosby Creek	1920	Howe	47
	37-20-28	Stewart	Mosby Creek	1930	Howe	48
	37-20-29	Brumbaugh	Mosby Creek	1948	Howe	49
	37-20-35	Ernest	Mohawk River	1938	Howe	50
	37-20-36	Wendling	Mill Creek	1938	Howe	51
	37-20-38	Deadwood	Deadwood Creek	1932	Howe	52
	37-20-40	Chambers	Coast Fork Willamette River	1936	Howe	53
	37-20-39	Office	N. F. Willamette	1944	Howe	54
Lincoln	37-21-02	Sam's Creek	Siletz River	1922	Howe	58
	37-21-03	Chitwood	Yaquina River	c. 1930	Howe	59
	37-21-05	Elk City	Yaquina River	1922	Howe	60
	37-21-08	N. Fork Yachats	N. Fork Yachats	1938	Queenpost	61
	37-21-11	Fisher	Five Rivers	1919	Howe	62
	37-21-14	Upper Drift Creek	Upper Drift Creek	1914	Howe	63
Linn	37-22-01	Jordan	Thomas Creek	1937	Howe	66
	37-22-02	Hannah	Thomas Creek	1936	Howe	67
	37-22-03	Shimanek	Thomas Creek	1966	Howe	68
	37-22-04	Gilkey	Thomas Creek	1939	Howe	69
	37-22-05	Weddle	Thomas Creek	1937	Howe	70
	37-22-06	Larwood	Crabtree Creek	1939	Howe	71
	37-22-07	Bohemian Hall	Crabtree Creek	1947	Howe	72
	37-22-08	Hoffman	Crabtree Creek	1936	Howe	73
	37-22-09	Short	S. Fork of the Santiam River	1945	Howe	74
	37-22-15	Crawfordsville	Calapooia River	1932	Howe	75
Marion	37-24-01	Gallon House	Abiqua Creek	1916	Howe	77
Polk	37-27-01	Ritner Creek	Ritner Creek	1927	Howe	80
	37-27-02	Pumping Station	Rickreall Creek	1915-16	Howe	81

GLOSSARY OF COVERED BRIDGE TERMS

Abutment—The foundation which supports the lower chord; usually constructed of concrete, timber, solid rock, or cribbing. The foundation at either end of the bridge, at the shore line.

Approach—The passage way from the road bed onto the bridge structure, usually of wood, gravel, concrete, or asphalt. The approach usually is enclosed on either side with guard rails, or fencing.

Bents—The vertical support for both pony truss and bridge span, usually set on footings.

Buttress—Reinforcement bracing from the wall onto an extension.

Chord—The long horizontal timber used either as the top or bottom truss member.

Daylighting—The method of allowing more light to enter the bridge structure, usually by a long narrow slit window above the truss top, sometimes the length of the bridge. Daylighting also allows faster drying of wet timbers.

Dead load—The acutual weight of the materials comprising the bridge.

Diagonal—The slanting timber truss member connecting the upper and lower chords.

Draw spans—Covered bridge designed to allow a portion, usually toward the center, to be raised to allow boats to pass.

End post—The diagonal at either end of a truss.

Floor beam—A supporting cross girder at the panel points under the stringers.

Foundation—The end supports for the bridge; the support for the lower chord, usually constructed of concrete, pilings, or rock. Foundations on shore are abutments, those between abutments are piers.

Hewn timber—Usually chords or truss members shaped by the use of hand tools.

Joists—The longitudinal supports under the flooring or planking to brace, and hold the flooring in place.

Lateral bracing—(cross bracing) Timber bracing horizontally strengthening and maintaining spacing of both trusses at the top and bottom of chords.

Lower chord—The long timber used as the bottom truss member; also stringer, or girder.

Piers—Foundation supports placed toward the center of the structure, generally used in multiple truss bridges.

Piling—Timber poles driven into the earth to form abutments, or piers, or a trestle.

Pony truss—A truss type which is lower than the height of passing loads, often as the approach to a bridge.

Portal—The openings at either end of the bridge. The use of a portal protects roof beams from the weather. Most portal styles are either rounded or square.

Portal weatherboarding—Wooden boarding inside the portal to protect the lower truss joints from water sprayed by traffic.

Rafter—The bracing to form the pitch of the roof, the boards to which the nailing strips are nailed to install the roof, either with shingles, or metal. The rafters form the peak at the roof and the other ends rest on the top truss or chord members.

Spliced timber—Two or more timber pieces joined end to end to form a single long chord.

Stringer—The longitudinal supporting joists under the floor planking.

Sway braces—The bracing either at the base of the bridge or at the roof line to strengthen the structure from moving during wind pressure, or from passing traffic. Sway braces can be flying buttresses, individually housed buttresses, or horizontal metal rods.

Tie rod—Vertical metal tension rods between the upper and lower chords, prevalent in Howe and queenpost trusses.

Trestle—A crossing supported entirely of timber poles or pilings in which a truss is not used to support weight.

Truss—A framework of diagonal members, forming a triangle or system of triangles to support the weight of the bridge as well as passing loads.

Tuning—The adustment of tie rods to maintain even tension on truss members.

Upper chord—The top truss member on all trusses, except kingpost trusses.

SELECTED BIOGRAPHY
Books and Journals:

Adams, Kramer. *Covered Bridges of the West*. Howell-North Books, Berkeley; 1963.

An Illustrated History of Union and Wallowa Counties. Western Historical Publishing Co., Spokane, Washington; 1902.

Bancroft, Hubert Howe. *History of Oregon*. (2 volumes) The Bancroft Company, New York; 1886; 1888.

Bridge Manual, Containing Standards, General Information and Instructions. Oregon State Highway Commission, Salem; 1916.

Covered Bridges in Oregon (pamphlet). Oregon State Highway Commission, Salem; 1952.

Dicken, Sam. *Pioneer Trails of the Oregon Coast*. Oregon Historical Society, Portland; 1971.

Farmer, Judith A. and Kenneth L. Holmes. *An Historical Atlas of Early Oregon*. Historical Cartographic Publications, Portland, Oregon; 1974.

Geer, Theodore T. *Fifty Years in Oregon*. Neale Publishing Company, New York; 1912.

History of the Willamette Valley, edited by H. O. Lang. G. H. Hines Co., Portland; 1885.

Horner, John B. *Oregon History and Early Literature*. The J. K. Gill Company, Portland, Oregon; 1919.

Illustrated History of Lane County. A. G. Walling Co., Portland, Oregon; 1884.

Journals, Local Laws and Joint Resolutions of the Legislative Assembly of the Territory of Oregon. Asahel Bush, Territorial Printer, Oregon City; 1855.

McArthur, Lewis B. *Oregon Geographic Names* (4th ed.). Oregon Historical Society, Portland, Oregon; 1974.

McCullough, C. B. *The Economics of Highway Bridge Types*. Gillette Publishing Co., Chicago; 1929.

Mullen, Floyd. *The Land of Linn.* Dalton's Printing Company, Lebanon, Oregon; 1971.

Nelson, Lee H. *A Century of Oregon Covered Bridges.* Oregon Historical Society, Portland, Oregon; 1960, 1976.

Oregon Covered Bridges (mimeographed). Oregon State Highway Division, Salem, Oregon; 1973.

Peterson, Emil R. and Alfred Powers. *A Century of Coos and Curry.* Binford and Mort Publishers, Portland, Oregon; 1952.

Sloane, Eric. *American Barns and Covered Bridges.* Wilfred Funk, Inc., New York; 1954.

World Guide to Covered Bridges, edited by Betsy and Philip Clough. The National Society for the Preservation of Covered Bridges, Reading, Massachusetts; 1959, 1972.

Also consulted were various county commissioners' journals and bridge maintenance logs.

Dillard Bridge: *This double Howe truss bridge over the South Umpqua River near Dillard was built under contract from the State Highway Commission in 1918. The bridge was daylighted by 4' x 8' windows until 1926 when a continuous window slit was made along each side, to enhance visibility. The span was damaged by high water in 1927 but was not replaced until the 1940's.*

Photo: Oregon Highway Commission

Periodicals:

Canby Herald
Capital Journal
Corvallis Gazette-Times
Covered Bridge Topics
Eugene Register Guard
Grants Pass Courier
Hillsboro Argus
Lane County Historian
Lincoln County Leader
Lowell Lakeside News
Oregon Spectator
Mollala Bulletin
Oregon Highway Commission Reports
Oregon Historical Quarterly
Oregonian
Oregon Journal (formerly Oregon State Journal)
Oregon Statesman
Stayton Mail
Springfield News
The Medford Mail-Tribune

The Authors

Wayne "Nick" Cockrell utilized his background of film and television production in co-authoring this volume on covered bridges. He has produced several short 16mm films, and while earning a graduate degree in Broadcast Communications at the University of Oregon, he taught several courses in film production. He had produced historical segments for educational television on such subjects as the Oregon Electric Railway, logging in early Oregon, and Luckey's Club Cigar Store, a cultural landmark in Eugene.

His interest in photography has been expressed in photographs of nature, sports, weddings and, of course, covered bridges. His other interests include hiking, sailing, cross country skiing and antique automobiles.

William "Bill" Cockrell added his photographic talents to his interest in covered bridges to produce some of the startling photographs of bridges in this volume. Although he initially studied civil engineering, he graduated from the University of Oregon with a degree in Business Administration.

His background in photography includes specialized courses from several photographic schools in the processing techniques of both color and black-and-white photographs, as well as other technical aspects of the medium of film. He has photographed college sports, weddings and architecture. He enjoys hiking, fishing, canoeing and photographing the vast Oregon outdoors.

Only the imprint of the rails indicates that the Chambers Bridge once handled trains instead of trucks. The actual use of the span was short. Built in 1936, to connect a logging spur to the Chambers Mill in Cottage Grove, the bridge experienced little use after the mill burned in 1943. The span is the sole remaining covered railroad bridge in Oregon. Time and progress have taken their toll on such structures which represent man's conquest of his environment and the settlement of the West.

Book design: Dean E. McMullen